ELECTED FRIENDS

ROBERT FROST & EDWARD THOMAS

TO ONE ANOTHER

ELECTED FRIENDS
ROBERT FROST & EDWARD THOMAS
TO ONE ANOTHER

Edited and with an Introduction by
MATTHEW SPENCER

Foreword by
MICHAEL HOFMANN

Afterword by
CHRISTOPHER RICKS

HANDSEL BOOKS

an imprint of
Other Press • New York

Production Editor: Robert D. Hack

This book was set in 11 pt. AGaramond by Alpha Graphics, Pittsfield, NH.

10 9 8 7 6 5 4 3 2 1

Library of Congress Cataloging-in-Publication Data

Frost, Robert, 1874-1963.
    Elected friends : Robert Frost and Edward Thomas to one another / edited by Matthew Spencer ; foreword by Michael Hofmann ; afterword by Christopher Ricks.
        p. cm.
Includes bibliographical references.
    ISBN 1-59051-083-6 (alk. paper)
    1. Frost, Robert, 1874-1963–Correspondence. 2. Frost, Robert, 1874-1963–Criticism and interpretation. 3. Poets, American–20th century–Correspondence. 4. Thomas, Edward, 1878-1917–Correspondence. 5. Authors, English–20th century–Correspondence. 6. Poets, Welsh–20th century–Correspondence. 7. Critics–Great Britain–Correspondence. 8. Thomas, Edward, 1878-1917–Poetry. 9. Frost, Robert, 1874-1963–Poetry. I. Thomas, Edward, 1878-1917. II. Spencer, Matthew. III. Title.
    PS3511.R94Z485 2003
    811'.52–dc22

                                                        2003017170
                                                        Rev.

ACKNOWLEDGMENTS

Handsel Books acknowledges Henry Holt and Company for the use of Robert Frost's poetry, and Peter Gilbert, head of the Frost archive at Dartmouth College. We remain indebted to the Edward Thomas Fellowship for their assistance, and especially to Myfanwy Thomas for her gracious permission to reprint her father's poems and letters.

Finally, the editor is grateful to the following friends and advisors for their generous help and criticism: Archie Burnett, David Ferry, Kenneth Haynes, Christopher Ricks, Stephen Sturgeon, and Harry Thomas. The editorial work was conducted under the auspices of the Editorial Institute at Boston University.

Table of Contents

EDITORIAL NOTE

Three of the letters in this book (18, 19, and 36) I have not seen in manuscript; I have reproduced the texts for these from Lawrance Thompson's *Selected Letters of Robert Frost*. Everywhere else I have tried to follow the manuscripts of the letters as closely as was practicable when preparing the texts. Cancelled words in the letters were in my judgment of little interest and therefore, in the other interest of the clean page, have not been included in the transcriptions. In all there are just over one hundred such cancellations in the manuscripts, and by far most of these were false starts (e.g., str, or at) rather than completed words. To avoid apparent misprints, I have supplied full stops in brackets wherever they are obviously missing in the manuscripts, numbering thirteen instances total. And I have similarly supplied obviously missing words and letters of words, numbering nine instances and four instances, respectively. I have also supplied one colon. Otherwise both the spelling and punctuation follow the manuscripts exactly. In the case of Thomas's letters, I have not indicated the curious gaps that often punctuate his sentences, though these can sometimes be of very great interest.

It should be noted of the correspondence printed here that it is an incomplete record. This is especially true of Frost's side of it. For it is clear from Thomas's letters that Frost wrote at least another eighteen letters to Thomas that I have been unable to locate. Though Frost admits to being a "bad letter writer" (August 15, 1916), he was not so bad a one as a glance through this book might suggest.

The texts of the poems, not including those that form parts of letters, are taken from R. George Thomas's edition of *The Collected Poems of Edward Thomas*, and from the Library of America's edition of Frost's *Collected Poems, Prose, & Plays*. The texts of Thomas's reviews of Frost and of his essay, "This England," are taken from Edna Longley's *A Language Not to Be Betrayed: Selected Prose of Edward Thomas*.

Numbers in boldface in the footnotes, for example [4], refer to the number of a letter, poem, or review included in this volume.

INTRODUCTION

I

This is an edition of the correspondence between the American poet Robert Frost and the English poet, critic, and journalist Edward Thomas. It includes not only their letters but also the poems that each wrote to or for the other, the three reviews that Thomas wrote of Frost's second volume of poems, *North of Boston*, and Thomas's essay, "This England," a small record of the time he spent with Frost at Ledington in August 1914 and of the fateful realization that began to crystallize in his mind during that time. It also includes one letter from Thomas to Frost's wife, Elinor, and two letters from Frost to Thomas's wife, Helen, in the second of which he very movingly expressed the intense grief that he felt after Thomas's death. Together these writings combine great literary interest with a greater human interest, documenting as they do both the thoughts of two important poets as well as the relationship of two remarkable friends.

For literary interest there is especially the story, in late 1914, of Thomas's blossoming as a poet, a blossoming due partly to Frost's genial and congenial influence. Overlapping with this story is that of Frost's achieving a long-sought-for critical recognition as a poet, for which he owed some thanks to Thomas and his three insightful reviews of *North of Boston*. By these reviews, as Frost later wrote to Grace Walcott Conkling, Thomas "gave me standing as a poet—

he more than anyone else"[1]; but Thomas also helped himself with these reviews, for his witnessing and testifying to what Frost had done for poetry helped him to firm up and give shape to critical inclinations he had been moving toward on his own for some time.

Intertwined with Thomas's poetic evolution is the humanly interesting story of his decision to enlist in the British Army—his evolution into "a conscious Englishman," as he put it to his friend Jesse Berridge in a letter dated September 3, 1914.[2] In August 1914, at the same time as Thomas was sending out his reviews of Frost's book, the Great War was breaking out in Europe. The war, and the ill-effects he knew the war would have on his ability to earn a living by his pen, his close friendship with an American, and the opportunity that came with this friendship of getting away from England and trying his luck for a time in America, all naturally led him to a reevaluation of what England meant, of who he was, and of what he needed to do. It all played a part in Thomas's becoming first a poet, and finally a soldier.

II

In the autumn of 1911 Robert Frost was newly a teacher of psychology and of the history of education at the New Hampshire State Normal School in Plymouth, New Hampshire. It had been about twenty years since he had published his first poem (in his high school newspaper), and he had been able to publish only a handful of efforts since. Now thirty-seven years of age and a father of four, he felt that poetry had better start working for him soon or he'd have to let go of its feet. As he put it around this time to his friend and former student John Bartlett, "it's the next three or four years, or never . . ."[3] He was even more precise in a letter of December 19,

---

[1] From a letter dated June 28, 1921, printed in *Poetry Wales*, vol. 13 no. 4 (Spring 1978), pp. 22–3.

[2] *The Letters of Edward Thomas to Jesse Berridge*, ed. Anthony Berridge (1983), p. 74.

[3] Quoted in Margaret Anderson, *Robert Frost and John Bartlett* (1963), p. 31.

1911 to his friend and benefactress Susan Hayes Ward, promising that his poetry's "forward movement is to begin next year."[4] By the end of 1912, the race would be on.

His new teaching position in Plymouth was one that he had accepted, according to his biographer Lawrance Thompson, "with the understanding that he might possibly resign . . . at the end of the year,"[5] for he had a notion to take advantage of an increased annuity from his grandfather's estate that was scheduled to take effect the following July. This, plus what money he could get from the sale of his grandfather's farm in Derry, which had recently become legally his to sell, would allow him some time to focus on his writing, some time free from the exhausting duties and pressures of teaching so as to give what was in him a chance to run. As he would later put it to Ernest Jewell, he felt the need "to be justified of my poetry. . . . I have hung off long enough. I wasn't going to pass forty without having it out with myself on this score . . ."[6]

With the summer of 1912 approaching, he began to feel that he'd better get away not only from teaching but also from local friends and family:

> I wanted to be as far away from the nosey relatives down Lawrence way as I could get, clear off. For by this time word had percolated down there that I was becoming a man of respectability, quite a change, perhaps I might even one day head up a big institution of learning. . . . They were good people who honestly were trying to save me from myself. I had no choice but to run away somewhere and hide.[7]

---

[4] *Selected Letters of Robert Frost*, ed. Lawrance Thompson (1964), p. 43.

[5] *Robert Frost: The Early Years* (1966), p. 367.

[6] From a letter dated May 6, 1913, quoted in Elizabeth Shepley Sergeant, *Robert Frost: The Trial by Existence* (1960), pp. 107–8.

[7] L. Mertins, *Robert Frost: Life and Talks-Walking* (1965), quoted in John Evangelist Walsh, *Into My Own* (1988), p. 31.

By August the choice of where to hide was between Vancouver, where John Bartlett was living, and England, where Frost's wife Elinor had long dreamed of living "under thatch." About mid-August the choice was made—by the toss of a coin. Frost's daughter Lesley later recalled the moment of decision:

> We were standing around my mother who was ironing in the kitchen when my father said, "Well, let's toss for it," and he took a nickel from his pocket. "Heads England, tails Vancouver." Heads it was! All that had been contemplated was fresh scenery, peace to write, the excitement of change.[8]

Two weeks later, with admirable whim, the Frosts were already on their way, sailing for England from Boston Harbor on August 23, 1912.

Frost was not alone in feeling that circumstances were keeping him from what he really wanted to do, and that sooner or later something would have to change for him. By 1911 Edward Thomas had established himself as a literary journalist worth listening to. But he was also buried in work that did not especially appeal to him and that paid little. Moreover, he often felt plagued by an imbalancing self-consciousness, which he described in a letter of December 1911 to his friend Harry Hooton:

> I have somehow lost my balance and can never recover it by diet or rule or any deliberate means, but only by some miracle from within or without. If I don't recover it and causes of worry continue I must go smash. . . . Sometimes I feel wellish here, sometimes very bad; never well, I never can be well again without the miracle.[9]

This intense dejection was nothing new for Thomas. A diary entry shows that he had arrived at similar strains of mind in the fall of 1907:

---

[8] Quoted in *Into My Own*, pp. 30–1.

[9] *Edward Thomas: Selected Letters*, ed. R. George Thomas (1995), pp. 68–9.

It is dislike of the effort to kill myself and fear that I could not carry it through if I half did it, that keeps me alive. Only that. For I hate my work, my reviewing: my best is negligible: I have no vitality, no originality, no love.[10]

The overbearing self-consciousness that seems to be at the root of it all does not, as the entry continues, escape Thomas's introspection:

I admire direct expressive natures . . . [the] voice, expressing likes and dislikes right out of his heart, without any of the hesitation which I have so often that I really never ought to say or write anything. . . . I believe I can be perfectly humble with a very young child, with no condescension or mere curiosity, simply responding to his emotions . . . and suggesting things to him which are inspired by him and would be impossible to me in a man's company, believing in things I say to this child more than I ever believe in what I write or what I say to Garnett for instance.[11]

Melancholy was such a consistent force in his life that, in 1913, he thought to accept a commission to write a book on ecstasy, feeling in a peculiar way qualified by "my intimate and long-standing a[c]quaintance with the opposite of ecstasy. I knew so well the 'grief without a pang' described with some flattery in Coleridge's Dejec-tion."[12] Unsurprisingly, perhaps, he found himself having difficulty staying on the topic while writing, and before long had to aban-don the work altogether.

In 1913 his letters to friends were often dismally black about his professional life. An undated letter written about this time to his friend Eleanor Farjeon spoke of "these days when to write more than a page means attempting the impossible and wearying myself

[10] Ibid., p. 44.

[11] Ibid., p. 45.

[12] Quoted in R. George Thomas, *Edward Thomas: A Portrait* (1985), pp. 254–5. Coleridge, "Dejection: An Ode," ll. 21–4: "A grief without a pang, void, dark, and drear, / A stifled, drowsy, unimpassioned grief, / Which finds no natural outlet, no relief, / In word, or sigh, or tear—"

and uselessly afflicting others with some part of my little yet endless tale."[13] He continually afflicted himself by dwelling on "all the distasteful work as if it were a great impossible mountain just ahead."[14] The problem was not how to get over the mountain, but how to get out from under it. He needed somehow to break the unending stream of literary work, for more and more he felt that "the kind of work I have had to do has paralysed me for original work except in short bursts . . ."[15] In the fall of 1913 he wrote to Harry Hooton that he sometimes got "wonderfully near deciding that it [literary work] shall not go on indefinitely, tho I don't see how to round it off."[16] What he needed—or at least what he got—was a "jog" from Robert Frost.[17]

Or perhaps it was something more than a jog. On October 5, 1913 Thomas wrote to Eleanor Farjeon a short letter of apology: "Will you forgive me if I do not turn up tomorrow? I have an appointment of uncertain time with an American just before & may not be able to come."[18] The American was, of course, the still largely unknown Robert Frost, and their meeting on October 6, 1913 may have been among the most important of their lives.

The meeting took place at St. George's Restaurant in St. Martin's Lane in London, a vegetarian restaurant that was a favorite haunt of Thomas's. It was arranged by the poet Ralph Hodgson, whose talents Thomas admired, and who was a regular attendant at the gatherings of writers that Thomas frequently presided over at St. George's. Hodgson had met Frost through the Georgian poet Wilfrid Gibson and had quickly thought to introduce Thomas to

---

[13] Eleanor Farjeon, *Edward Thomas: The Last Four Years* (1958), p. 13.

[14] Ibid.

[15] *Edward Thomas: Selected Letters*, p. 95.

[16] Ibid., p. 86.

[17] The word, quite a happy one, is F. R. Leavis's, in "The Fate of Edward Thomas," *Scrutiny* (March 1939), p. 442: "As a poet, of course, he got his jog from Robert Frost . . ."

[18] *Edward Thomas: The Last Four Years*, p. 37.

the American after being impressed by Frost's "The Death of the Hired Man," which Frost was circulating in manuscript about this time. There seems nothing to know about this first meeting aside from its having happened. Hodgson and others may have also been present, but this is uncertain. The meeting evidently came off happily enough, but I've seen no other testimony than that they bothered to meet again—though not until mid-December. (Thomas's letter to Frost confirming this meeting, dated December 17, 1913, is the earliest that survives.)

Over the next year, by R. George Thomas's accounting, Frost and Thomas "spent the equivalent of six or seven weeks together."[19] Very few details about their meetings have been recorded, but it seems clear that the friendship grew quickly. For by the end of January, when Thomas was thinking of spending some time in the country, he was hoping to find a place to stay that would be near to Frost. (He wrote to him on January 30, "I don't quite know where I shall go, but if you happen to know any really cheap lodgings in your part of the country will you tell me?") And by the end of March, Eleanor Farjeon reports, Thomas had begun "to talk about his friend, and was drawn after him as by a magnet. . . . Frost had already shown Edward 'The Death of the Hired Man' in manuscript, and wherever they were together the great endless talk on poetry was pursued."[20]

But it was not just the "talk on poetry" that ballasted their friendship. There was a deeper human connection beyond the literary talk in which they delighted. Frost wrote to Edward Garnett shortly after Thomas's death: "Edward Thomas was the only brother I ever had."[21] Thomas felt attracted to and at ease with the bluff personality of Frost; he gladly reported to Eleanor Farjeon on their activities during a visit he paid to Frost: "We loaf and talk."[22] And he would

[19] "Edward Thomas and Robert Frost," in *Poetry Wales*, vol. 13. no. 4 (Spring 1978), p. 24.

[20] *Edward Thomas: The Last Four Years*, p. 65.

[21] *Selected Letters of Robert Frost*, p. 217.

[22] *Edward Thomas: The Last Four Years*, p. 100.

later confess to Frost that he was the only person he could be idle with.[23] He described the idling that took place during a month-long visit of August 1914 in an article he wrote for *The Nation*:

> How easy it was to spend a morning or afternoon in walking over to his [Frost's] house, stopping to talk to whoever was about for a few minutes, and then strolling with my friend, nearly regardless of footpaths, in a long loop, so as to end either at his house or at my lodging. . . . If talk dwindled in the traversing of a big field, the pause at the gate or stile braced it again. Often we prolonged the pause, whether we actually sat or not, and we talked—of flowers, childhood, Shakespeare, women, England, the war—or we looked at the far horizon, which some dip or gap occasionally disclosed.[24]

Years later, writing the second of her two memoirs, Helen Thomas remembered their remarkable friendship as well as its remarkable effect:

> Between him and Edward a most wonderful friendship grew up. He believed in Edward and loved him, understanding, as no other man had ever understood, his strange complex temperament. The influence of this man on Edward's intellectual life was profound, and to it alone of outside influences is to be attributed that final and fullest expression of himself which Edward now found in writing poetry.[25]

And to his friendship with Thomas, of outside influences, is to be attributed the extraordinary character of Frost's final year in England, which he recalled for Amy Lowell in October 1917:

> I don't know that I ever told you, but the closest I ever came in friendship to anyone in England or anywhere else in the world I think was with

---

[23] [22], p. 52.

[24] "This England," [15], p. 31.

[25] *World Without End*, p. 152.

Edward Thomas who was killed at Vimy last spring. He more than any-one else was accessory to what I had done and was doing. We were to-gether to the exclusion of every other person and interest all through 1914—1914 was our year. I never had, I never shall have another such year of friendship.[26]

III

To Frost's influence "alone of outside influences," Helen Thomas attributed "that final and fullest expression of himself Edward now found in writing poetry." At the end of 1914, after years of barely making a less-than-decent living as a writer and literary journal-ist, and finding himself more and more having to take on hack work, Edward Thomas discovered that he was a poet after all. He wrote his first poem, "Up in the Wind," in early Decem-ber 1914. It had been a little over a year since he had first met Robert Frost, and since his other new friend, Eleanor Farjeon, had asked him whether he had ever written any poetry and he had an-swered: "Me? . . . I couldn't write a poem to save my life."[27] But in May 1914 Thomas wrote to Frost, with charming timidity, "I wonder whether you can imagine me taking to verse. If you can I might get over the feeling that it is impossible . . ."[28] Im-possible it would be to say just where this wondering came from. Frost's own feeling was that he had been suppressing this aspira-tion his whole life: "It was plain that he had wanted to be a poet all the years he had been writing about poets not worth his little finger."[29]

No written reply from Frost to this letter survives—it may be that he never wrote one—but he did not lose the opportunity to

---

[26] *Selected Letters of Robert Frost*, p. 220.

[27] *Edward Thomas: The Last Four Years*, p. 41.

[28] [7], p. 10.

[29] To Grace Walcott Conkling, June 28, 1921, op. cit., p. 23.

encourage his friend. We have Frost's own testimony as to how this encouragement was administered:

> He was throwing to his big perfunctory histories of Marlborough and the like written to order such poetry as would make him a name if he were but given credit for it. I made him see that he owed it to himself and the poetry to have it out by itself in poetic form where it must suffer itself to be admired.[30] It took me some time. I bantered, teased and bullied all the summer we were together at Ledington and Ryton. All he had to do was put his poetry in a form that declared itself. The theme must be the same, the accent exactly the same. He saw it and was tempted. It was plain that he had wanted to be a poet all the years he had been writing about poets not worth his little finger. But he was afeared (though a soldier). His timidity was funny and fascinating. I had about given him up, he had turned his thoughts to enlistment and I mine to sailing for home when he wrote his first poem.[31]

Frost's encouragement was timely because Thomas would no longer have opportunities for literary journalism after the war broke out in August. His life had to change, and it did: he wrote his first poem in early December; he would enlist several months later. He was killed in the Battle of Arras on April 9, 1917. His last letter to Frost was written a week before. Their surviving correspondence, over three and a half years, is a record of a warm friendship, of the growth of two friends, and of the growth of two poets.

Matthew Spencer

---

[30] Alluding to Waller's "Go, lovely rose," ll. 11–5: "Small is the worth / Of beauty from the light retired; / Bid her come forth, / Suffer herself to be desired, / And not blush so to be admired."

[31] To Grace Walcott Conkling, June 28, 1921, printed in *Poetry Wales*, vol. 13 no. 4 (Spring 1978), p. 23.

CHRONOLOGY

1912

August 23   Frost sails for England with family from Boston Harbor.

September 2   Frost arrives at Glasgow on the *Parisian*.

September 15   Frost living at The Bungalow, in Beaconsfield.

October 26   Frost receives note from Mrs. Nutt that *A Boy's Will* has been accepted for publication.

1913

January 8   Frost attends opening evening at Monro's Poetry Bookshop, where he meets F. S. Flint, who later introduces him to Ezra Pound.

c. April 1   *A Boy's Will* is published.

July   Thomas family moves from Wick Green to Yew Tree Cottage, in the village of Steep, near Petersfield.

August   Frost meets Wilfrid Gibson.

c. September 14 Frost meets Ralph Hodgson.

October 6   Frost and Thomas meet for the first time, at St. George's Restaurant in London.

December 22   Frost and Thomas meet for the second time, again at St. George's.

1914

February	Thomas receives Royal Literary Fund grant.
March 24	Thomas visits Frost at The Bungalow.
April	Frost, entreated by Abercrombie and Gibson, moves to Little Iddens in Ledington.
	Thomas publishes *In Pursuit of Spring.*
April 25–May 2	Thomas visits Frost at Little Iddens.
May 15	Frost publishes *North of Boston.*
June 24–27	Thomas visits Frost at Little Iddens, from where he reports to Eleanor Farjeon, "It is splendid here, every day hot and bright."
July	Thomas visits Frost at Little Iddens.
August	Thomas publishes three reviews of *North of Boston.*
August c. 3–26	Thomas family visits Frost family at Little Iddens, lodging nearby at the Chandlers' farm.
September	Frost moves to The Gallows in Ryton, Gloucestershire.
October 15–19	Thomas visits Frost at The Gallows. He reports to Eleanor Farjeon, "Now I am idling and making notes for another English Review article—on what country people say about the war and its effects. . . . The children are well here but Mrs. Frost tired and Robert not very well. It is languid still weather which I enjoy completely. . . . We loaf and talk."
November	Thomas begins writing verse.
November 25–c. 30	Thomas visits Frost at The Gallows, where they have a disagreeable experience with a local gamekeeper.

1915

February 10	Frost visits Thomas at Steep.
February 13	Frost family sails from Liverpool with Mervyn Thomas on the American ship *St. Paul.*
February 22	Frosts arrive in New York. Elinor and the children

	retire to the Lynches' farm in Bethlehem, New Hampshire.
February	Frost spends time in New York and Boston, meeting editors and other literary figures.
April	Frost finds farm in Franconia.
June	Frost family moves to Franconia farm, after a hitch in the sale is resolved.
July 14	Thomas passed for military service by doctor.
July 19	Thomas enlists in the Artist's Rifles. Billeted in Balham with parents.
October	Thomas moves to camp at High Beech.
November	Thomas moves to Hare Hall Camp and is promoted to lance corporal.
c. November 30	Elinor Frost's pregnancy ends in miscarriage.

1916

May	Thomas promoted to full corporal.
June	Thomas awarded Civil List grant.
September	Frost sends some of Thomas's poems to Harriet Monroe, editor of *Poetry*.
	Thomas sent to the Royal Artillery school in London.
October	Thomas family moves from Steep to High Beech.
	Thomas at firing camp, Trowbridge.
November	Thomas made 2nd lieutenant. Posted to RGA Lydd, Kent.
	Frost publishes *Mountain Interval*.

1917

January	Thomas at Codford for firing practice.
	Frost begins teaching at Amherst College.
January 29	Thomas leaves for France.
April 9	Thomas killed at Observation Post in Battle of Arras.

BIOGRAPHICAL TABLE

Abercrombie, Lascelles (1881–1938) Poet and critic. Friend and neighbor of Wilfrid Gibson. In 1914 he invited the Frosts to live near him (and Gibson) in Gloucestershire; later in the same year he invited them to share his own cottage.

Bottomley, Gordon (1874–1948) Poet and dramatist. Close friend of Thomas, whose letters to him were published by Oxford University Press in 1968 (ed. R. George Thomas).

Brooke, Rupert (1887–1915) Poet. Friend of Abercrombie and Gibson. Died during the war.

Davies, W. H. (1871–1940) Poet and friend of Thomas.

De la Mare, Walter (1873–1956) Poet, novelist, and friend of Thomas.

Ellis, Vivian Locke Poet, editor, and friend of Thomas, who occasionally stayed at his home as a paying guest.

Farjeon, Eleanor (1881–1965) Writer and close friend of Thomas family. Author of *Edward Thomas: The Last Four Years* (1958). Often helped Thomas type his poems and send them out to editors.

Flint, F. S. (1885–1960) Poet, acquaintance of Frost, through whom he met Ezra Pound.

Freeman, John (1880–1929) Poet and critic. Friend of Thomas.

Garnett, Edward (1868–1937) Critic, editor, dramatist, and friend of Thomas.

Gibson, Wilfrid (1878–1962) Poet, friend, and neighbor of Abercrombie. Introduced Frost to Ralph Hodgson, who in turn introduced him to Thomas.

Haines, Jack Solicitor, botanist, poet. Friend of Frost and of Thomas.

Hodgson, Ralph (1871–1962) Poet and friend of Thomas.

Hodson, C. F. Master at Bedales School, near Thomas's cottage at Steep, and later at Bablake School in Coventry, where Mervyn Thomas went to study in 1915. Friend of Thomas.

Hudson, W. H. (1841–1922) Prolific writer and friend of Thomas.

Hulme, T. E. (1883–1917) Aesthetic philosopher associated with Pound. Interested in Frost's ideas about sentence sounds. Died in the war.

Marsh, Sir Edward (1872–1953) Influential London editor. Coined the term "Georgian Poetry," and edited each of the five volumes of the *Georgian Poetry* anthology (published by Monro).

Monro, Harold (1879–1932) Editor of *Poetry and Drama* (1913–14), to which Thomas contributed. In 1913 he founded the Poetry Bookshop in London, where Frost made some of his first literary contacts in England. Published Sir Edward Marsh's anthologies of *Georgian Poetry*.

Radford, Maitland Doctor and friend of Thomas.

Scott, Russell Nephew of the journalist C. P. Scott. Friend of Thomas family from Bedales School, where he was junior master. Went to America in 1914, where in 1915 he played host to the visiting Mervyn Thomas.

Scott-James, R. A. (1878–1959) Journalist, editor, critic. Editor of *The New Weekly*, a literary journal to which Thomas contributed.

Trevelyan, R. C. (1872–1951) Poet and translator. Friend of Bottomley and editor of *An Anthology of New Poetry* (1918), which printed some of Thomas's poems along with some of Frost's.

BIBLIOGRAPHY

Anderson, M. B. (1963). *Robert Frost and John Bartlett: The Record of a Friendship*. New York: Holt, Rinehart and Winston.

Cooke, W. (1970). *Edward Thomas: A Critical Biography 1878–1917*. London: Faber and Faber.

Coombes, H. (1973). *Edward Thomas: A Critical Study*. New York: Barnes and Noble.

Eckert, R. P. (1937). *Edward Thomas: A Biography and a Bibliography*. New York: E. P. Dutton & Co.

Evans, W. R. (1981). *Robert Frost and Sidney Cox: Forty Years of Friendship*. Hanover, New Hampshire: University Press of New England.

Farjeon, E. (1958). *Edward Thomas: The Last Four Years*. New York: Oxford University Press.

Francis, L. L. (1994). *The Frost Family's Adventure in Poetry: Sheer Morning Gladness at the Brim*. Columbia: University of Missouri Press.

Frost, R. (1963). *The Letters of Robert Frost to Louis Untermeyer*, ed. Louis Untermeyer. New York: Holt, Rinehart and Winston.

——— (1964). *Selected Letters of Robert Frost*, ed. Lawrance Thompson. New York: Holt, Rinehart and Winston.

——— (1995). *Collected Poems, Prose, & Plays*, ed. Richard Poirier and Mark Richardson. New York: The Library of America.

——— (1997). *Interviews with Robert Frost*, ed. Edward Connery Lathem. Guilford, Connecticut: Jeffrey Norton.

Hart, L. (1998). "The Only Brother I Ever Had." *Acumen*, no. 30, January, pp. 20–26.

——— (2000). *Once They Lived in Gloucestershire: A Dymock Poets Anthology*. Gloucestershire: Green Branch.

Leavis, F. R. (1932). *New Bearings in English Poetry*. Ann Arbor: The University of Michigan Press, 1960.

——— (1939). "The Fate of Edward Thomas." *Scrutiny*, vol. vii, no. 4, March, pp. 441–443.

Lehmann, J. (1983). *Three Literary Friendships*. New York: Quartet Books.

Moore, J. (1939). *The Life and Letters of Edward Thomas*. London: William Heinemann Ltd.

Pritchard, W. H. (1984). *Frost: A Literary Life Reconsidered*. New York: Oxford University Press.

Scannell, V. (1963). *Edward Thomas*. London: Longmans, Green & Co.

Sergeant, E. S. (1960). *Robert Frost: The Trial by Existence*. New York: Holt, Rinehart and Winston.

Thomas, E. (1968). *Letters from Edward Thomas to Gordon Bottomley*, ed. R. George Thomas. London: Oxford University Press.

——— (1973). *Poems and Last Poems*, ed. Edna Longley. London: Collins Publishers.

——— (1978). *The Collected Poems of Edward Thomas*, ed. R. George Thomas. Oxford: Clarendon Press.

——— (1981). *A Language Not to Be Betrayed: Selected Prose of Edward Thomas*. ed. Edna Longley. New York: Persea Books.

——— (1983). *The Letters of Edward Thomas to Jesse Berridge*, ed. Anthony Berridge. London: Enitharmon Press.

——— (1995). *Selected Letters*, ed. R. George Thomas. Oxford: Oxford University Press.

Thomas, H. *Under Storm's Wing*. London: Paladin Books, 1990.

Thomas, R. G. (1968). "Edward Thomas, Poet and Critic." *Essays and Studies*, pp. 118–136.

——— (1972). *Edward Thomas*. Cardiff: University of Wales Press.

——— (1978). "Edward Thomas and Robert Frost." *Poetry Wales*, vol. 13 no. 4, Spring, pp. 24–41.

——— (1985). *Edward Thomas: A Portrait*. Oxford: Clarendon Press.

Thompson, L., and Winnick, R. H. (1966). *Robert Frost: The Early Years 1874–1915*. New York: Holt, Rinehart and Winston.

———— *Robert Frost: The Years of Triumph 1915–1938*. (1970). New York: Holt, Rinehart and Winston.

Thornton, R. (1937). *Recognition of Robert Frost: Twenty-Fifth Anniversary*. New York: Henry Holt and Company.

Wain, J. (1978). "Edward Thomas and Helen Thomas." *Professing Poetry*, pp. 224–255. New York: Penguin.

Walsh, J. E. (1988). *Into My Own: The English Years of Robert Frost 1912–1915*. New York: Grove Press.

FOREWORD

"I thought all the mails had gone down in the Laconic, but evidently not."
Helen Thomas to Robert Frost, 2 March 1917

Parnassian friendships—in particular friendships between poets—are rarer than one might imagine. A friendship late in life is unlikely, poets are so botanically specialized and overdetermined, each one stuck at the extremity of his or her personal development, craning and twisting apotropaically toward his or her personal light. Early friendships are subject to volatility, the vicissitudes of life, and the torque—or torc—of the muse. When one has further taken away such things as alliances (Pound and Eliot), dalliances (Lowell and Bishop), rivalries (Goethe and Schiller), dependencies (Spender and Auden), romantic entanglements (Verlaine and Rimbaud), and mentor–pupil relationships (Akhmatova and Brodsky), one is left with really not very many. Where so much in a poet's life is either contingency or duress, the "elected" element proudly stressed in the title of this exceptional collection is whittled right down.

Montaigne's marvelously, irreducibly simple formulation for friendship, *"Parce que c'etait lui, parce que c'etait moi,"*—"because it was him, because it was me"—can have few juster claimants among poets than Robert Frost (1874–1963) and Edward Thomas (1878–1917). Friendship is such a mystery (and therefore such a provocation—a diaphanous rag to a bull) that it's no surprise critics have queued up to explain this instance of it, but it doesn't come down to such things as more or less one-sided influencings, or Linda

Hart's impressively foolish list of congruencies, such things as Hampshire / New Hampshire. For Frost, who outlived by the best part of half a century the friend he saw for one year, and wrote to for another two, the relationship was unrepeatable and irreplaceable. For Thomas, it was both an enabling agency—but for it, we might never have read him, or even heard of him—and an object of intensest focus. One could do worse, as one reads through the letters, poems, and reviews assembled here, than murmur Montaigne's words to oneself from time to time.

A starting-point better than the second-guessing and computer-matchmaking of some of the critics is to understand that the friendship between Frost and Thomas came about, in a strange way, out of time and out of place. This creates the space for some of its electiveness. Frost, evidently, was not in his own country but in the England he had bravely and arbitrarily plumped for a year earlier, nor did Thomas have home advantage either. Often, he was guesting in his hated London, touting for work ("I hate meeting people I want to get something out of, perhaps." 23 May 1915), or else, in the Edwardian fashion, passing himself around like the port among various addresses. (Eleanor Farjeon he met in the course of a "cricket week".) In fact, if one imagines, in one of P. G. Wodehouse's "Psmith" novels, a meeting in a London chophouse or a country pile—say, Blandings in Shropshire—and a fast friendship being formed between Psmith's likable friend Mike Jackson and—not Psmith, but instead Ralston McTodd, "the powerful singer of Saskatoon"—I don't think the story of Frost and Thomas is altogether unlike a serious version of that. Even when they were living in adjacent cottages, in Ledington and Ryton, Thomas didn't know that particular bit of country (not far from the imaginary Blandings); there was a local hill from which he could see Wales, but basically, he was no more "at home" there than the American visitor.

Nor could either man draw on the authority of years, family, accomplishments. True, they both had their families—Frost with his four children, Thomas his three—but to some extent, both were on the run from them. They were both in settled, or serious years, mid- to late-thirties—Frost the older by four years, and seeming older than that, I would guess, by virtue of being American and having traveled, of having grown up half-orphaned, of having come into money from his grandfather—but neither had very much to show for their time on earth, and both were well aware of the fact. If anything, Thomas, who was a hugely prolific and hard-working literary journalist, with a string of books to his name, should have had the upper hand on an erstwhile farmer and occasional teacher, an idle and irascible man who had barely published anything—only he saw in his own extensive production chiefly grounds for shame. (In fact, he was a wonderful writer of prose: the original texts have long since disappeared from sale, and even selections like Roland Gant's *Edward Thomas on the Countryside* and Edna Longley's *A Language Not to Be Betrayed* are not easy to find, but they are all worth the trouble: marvelously alert and rapturous prose.) Both Frost and Thomas had the discontents and aspirations of much younger men, though both, evidently, had seen and experienced far more of life. This strange mixing of ages characterized them, separately and together. On the one hand, the immoderateness and capacity and ebullience of youth, and youth's faith in friendship's great exchange, and on the other, the urgency and narrowing purpose of midlife, what the Germans call *Torschlusspanik* ("fear of the gate closing"). It was one of the conditions of their friendship, the inability of either man to be his age. They were unfinished, unappreciated, adrift, and thrown together.

Their time, their era, too, left them alone. The whole beginning of the twentieth century was in a somewhat similar muddle to themselves, a sort of soft interregnum. It was old and young, and it didn't have long to go. Historians don't know quite what to do with it; often, they simply add those fourteen years to the nineteenth century, as if that was where they really belonged. The great reputations—James, Hardy, Yeats—had all been founded in the Victorian age. When Frost's favorite living poet died in 1909, it was George Meredith. The reputations of the 1900s and 1910s, of the Edwardians and Georgians, (those characters listed in Matthew Spencer's *Biographical Table*—I would almost call it a glossary!) have disappeared more thoroughly than those of any other decade. No one now reads those poets Edward Thomas spent a great part of his lifetime sifting in the *Daily Chronicle*. And against that, the Modern had pushed its foot in the door. "On or about December 1910," as Virginia Woolf would have us believe, "human nature changed." Lawrence is a dangerous presence, Pound is at home in London—"sometimes," as he wrote on his visiting card to a predictably nettled and crestfallen Frost—and the soon-to-be imagists Flint and Hulme are there to be met, and always our knowledge of the impending War. It is a confused and unimpressive waiting, the situation of Saul Bellow's first book, *Dangling Man*, George Orwell's *Coming Up for Air*, or Julian Maclaren-Ross's *Of Love and Hunger*.

In this brief abeyance, the friendship took hold and grew. They met twice in 1913; 1914 was "their year"; in February 1915, the Frosts sailed (taking with them, as a kind of wonderful pledge or earnest, Thomas's oldest child, Mervyn or Merfyn); Thomas started to write poems and enlisted, Elinor Frost suffered ill health and a miscarriage, Frost embarked on his prodigious career as a professional bard and performer ("Dear Edward: First I want to give you an accounting." 15 August 1916). Everything is changed; changed utterly. This was, for all involved (even, one suspects, the onlookers), a transformative relationship. The plot has the bold X-shape of a perfect short story (say, Chekhov's "Lady with Lapdog"—and, indeed, the friendship has absolutely the intensity of an affair).

This "story"—a kind of natural, unprocessed narration, with beginning, middle, and end—is most exquisitely set off, or inverted, by the epistolary form. Because there can be no doubt that its deepest moments were when the two men were together at Ledington, improvising walks and conversations. It was not in its essence a written (or even primarily a *literary*, except inasmuch as both men were literary) relationship at all—not *Fernliebe*, heady and disinhibited—but one founded on time eagerly and intensely spent together, and it is of precisely this that we are necessarily ignorant. First names—the *tu* or *Du* form that registers electrically upon a European ear—are only used once the Atlantic has come between the writers. Intimacy, perhaps, to redress distance. Strikingly, and sadly, there seems not to be a single photograph—what one might jokingly call prima facie evidence—of the two men together. A handful of poems (one by the awful Gibson), a few paragraphs of recollection from the principals, and by Helen Thomas and Eleanor Farjeon. What is proposed to us is the form of an arch, but all we see of it are the respective beginnings or foundations. We see the men building toward each other. The middle, their meeting, eludes our inquisitiveness. Letters are predicated upon absence; in an extreme instance of this, one single letter from Frost to Thomas seems to have survived from the time before his departure. They have a natural, aleatory tact, very much in keeping with the characters of both men. In her wonderful memoir, *As It Was*, Helen Thomas wrote of Edward: "For though he needed and loved my impulsive and demonstrative nature, these qualities were foreign to him" (p. 66). Frost, meanwhile, wrote on 26 June 1915 to Thomas: "I have passionately regretted exposing myself,"—though not to Thomas.

Precisely because of what one might call its refusal of distance, though, the collection displays a characteristic and very appealing exaggeration, blandishment, almost flirtatiousness. Again, this is supplied almost as much by what isn't there—the "silence" from Frost, which of course isn't a real silence—as by what is: Thomas's tireless charm, solicitude, address, seductiveness. There is just no way for him *to be* without his friend, and Frost's absence or unavailability leads him—almost from the beginning, "Dear Frost (if you don't mind)"—to the brink of excess, impropriety, fantasy, whatever one wants to call it. The early notes from Thomas seem to live always toward their next meeting, to sigh, almost romantically, for more favorable conditions, where cake can be had and eaten: "There must be a world where that is done. I hope you & I will meet in it" (19 May 1914). He is like a man pressing his suit upon some chilly fair, or even—such is the force of so much charm, desire, wistfulness—a woman. In 1910 Thomas had published a book called *Feminine Influence on the Poets*; "till I got to his signature," he writes of Richard Burton in #38, "I thought he was a she" (p. 91); his concluding presentations of himself are regularly "feminine": "but you know already how much I waver & on what wavering things I depend" (p. 8), the odalisque-like "It is purely disinclination to sprawl about before your eyes as I feel I should do, more than usual, just now" (p. 15), or the frankly eye-rolling "If you were there I might even break away from the Duke for 3 days, but it would be hard" (p. 52). (I'm sure I overstate Thomas's femininity. It's just my somewhat coarse approximation for the combination of youth, pliancy, respect, and teasing that he offers Frost. And of course, with his "strength and silence," Frost plays his male part.)

All this, of course, is not to suggest there was any homoerotic component in the relationship, but rather to propose that something of what one thinks of as merely or exclusively sexual—the gallantry or flirtatiousness of seduction—inheres in many, if not most, great friendships. In fact, I would say there is something a little strange where it's not there. There is something, in Robert Lowell's words, "too little nonsensical" even in the twinkle of Brecht's invitation to Walter Benjamin to share his Danish exile with him: "How's your health? How about a trip to the northland? The chess board lies orphaned; every half hour a tremor of remembrance runs through it; that was when you made your moves." There is something deliberate and deflected and third person neuter about this; too much depends on the cartoon-animated chessboard; it is not torrid but cool, witty-whimsical rather than charming, and seems already to accept the possibility of defeat. Thomas, by contrast, like the heroine of a bodice-ripper, seems always ready to hurl himself quixotically against any let or hindrance: to walk anywhere, cycle any distance, use any pretext, accept any lodging. It's as though he always has their respective coordinates plotted on a map, and has in his pocket a compass with Frost his true north. And in this, he is even occasionally—happily!—outdone by a still more exorbitant Frost, who makes the amazing suggestion that Thomas take a little three-week leave of absence from the army and cross the Atlantic to talk to him. After all, he says, reasonably (because reason also is part of the process!), "They ought to consider that you were literary before you were military" (6 November 1916). The assertion of primacy, like the—naked or exaggerated or (to the writer) surely irresistible—expression of need, seems to me a term from love's lexicon.

The romance of friendship is to me a very beguiling trait in these letters. And while Thomas, who wrote most of the letters that have come down to us—and most of the longer letters at that—seems to make most of the running, this is an accidental impression (although it is one of the minor pleasures of reading this collection deliberately to entertain it). Frost's letters may be less engagingly volatile—less *frisky*, almost, than Thomas's—but rarely can he have come over as so attractively involved as he does here; one cannot say with any degree of confidence that "the more loving one"—Auden—is Thomas. Rather, dangling before his friend such heavenly and Kafka-ishly impossible notions as the "lecture-camp" in New Hampshire, Frost entered fully into the solicitous optimism of the relationship.

At the same time, most movingly, Thomas quit it. It's as though the torch of hope and ambition (and illusion) had passed from him to Frost. In his last two years of soldiering and poetry, he seems to move, quite consciously, into an unreachable final solitude. At the end of a tightening spiral—shorter, more "mannish" sentences, less self-reflection and self-censure, renunciation (of Steep, of reading, of friendship, of the idea of a future), the affirmation of more and more negatively couched perspectives—there is only death. "All the anchors are up," he writes on 9 September 1916. He sees himself in a sort of continual masquerade, in strange, tight clothes, an artilleryman's moustache, rising through spectral ranks, a dirty somnambulist, and yet—absurdly—a schoolmasterly figure among much younger men, quite unrecognized ["I wonder would you recognise me with hair cropped close & carrying a thin little swagger cane" (13 November 1915); "Nobody recognises me now" (21 May 1916); "my disguises increase, what with spurs on my heels & hair on my upper lip" (19 October 1916)] to the point where he simultaneously becomes himself and doesn't know himself. ("*Niemand, der mich kennt*"—"no one knows who I am"—are Rilke's dying words.) Thomas seems to rebalance himself in negation. Frost, meanwhile, is a tender irrelevance, not quite knowing whether to cheer from the sidelines of American neutrality—very much as at a sports event—to praise the personality of Lloyd George, to recall old memories of their times together, to envy Thomas's uncomfortable mastery of "black talk," or to give him an anxious shaking: "Don't be run away with by your nonsense" (23 November 1915). Many of these pages are at the extremity of friendship.

I haven't talked much about poetry. Poetry seems to come naturally and variously out of the relationship. It is Frost telling his friend that of course he can imagine him "taking to verse." It is both in Thomas's sublimely candid and intelligent reviews of *North of Boston,* and in his bantering references to "North of Bostonism" in his own work. ("Influence" seems to me such a ridiculously, barbarously heavy notion here: I don't think Thomas set himself to write Frost poems any more than Frost set himself to write Thomas poems. Thomas may be vastly less known than Frost—especially in the United States—but I don't think he has anything to fear from the comparison. Rather, I should say that their poems, as I should take it their wives and their children, were on friendly terms with one another.) It is Frost sending Thomas "The Road Not Taken"—

and I don't suppose anyone who reads it in such a context will ever view Frost or the poem in the same way again. It is Thomas taking exception to the closing line of a poem, and his discreetest reservations about plays, about plainness, and—less discreetly—about things being "made up" or "thought out" (10 June 1916) or "done too much on purpose" (19 October 1916). It is in innumerable felicities of expression one finds on the wayside, as it were, in these letters, such as Thomas's feeling "thinned out by reading and smoking"; or his writing about "little trees & some great pears," and wishing Frost, in an utterly Keatsish way, "I hope you have some as good, so that you can eat them till your teeth are sad with them," (12 October 1915); his comparing "a foxhunting major" to "a mandrill" (4 October 1915) (though what else is an officer, if not someone who drills men?); it is Frost's astonishing unpunctuated, inverted, unquestioning question: "For what has a man locomotion if it isnt to take him into things he is between barely and not quite understanding" (31 July 1915). It is Thomas saying, "I could read Frost, I think" (31 December 1916), and later, in his last letter, revising this—you see, these really aren't bookish letters—assuring his friend: "yet you are no more like an American in a book than you were 2½ years ago" (2 April 1917).

Michael Hofmann
London, July 2003

ABBREVIATIONS

AP	*Edward Thomas: A Portrait*
CPET	*The Collected Poems of Edward Thomas*
CPPP	Robert Frost, *Collected Poems, Prose, & Plays*
EF	*Edward Thomas: The Last Four Years*
ETSL	*Edward Thomas: Selected Letters*
GB	*Letters from Edward Thomas to Gordon Bottomley*
IMO	*Into My Own: The English Years of Robert Frost*
JB	*The Letters of Edward Thomas to Jesse Berridge*
SLRF	*Selected Letters of Robert Frost*
TEY	*Robert Frost: The Early Years*
YOT	*Robert Frost: The Years of Triumph*

THE TEXTS

I. 1913–1914

1. Thomas to Frost[1]

at Selsfield House[2]

17 xii 13   *East Grinstead*

Dear Frost (if you don't mind)

I shall be glad to see you again & Flint for the first time on Monday next at St George's[3] at 4. You remember the place in St Martin's Lane where we first met.[4] Top floor. I think Davies & Hodgson will be there.

Yours sincerely
E Thomas.

---

[1] Written on a letter card addressed to "Robert Frost Esq. / The Bungalow / Beaconsfield / Buckinghamshire." On the back of the letter card Thomas wrote, "In case I forgot to mention it / 4 O'clock is the time I propose."

[2] The home of Vivian Locke Ellis in East Sussex, where Thomas stayed from early December through January 15.

[3] A favorite restaurant of Thomas's in London.

[4] On October 6, 1913.

2. Thomas to Frost[1]

at Selsfield House
East Grinstead

I am going to be at St George's both next Friday & the Wednesday after at 4. Can you come either day or both? In any case I hope you have no cold to prevent you. Wednesday might be the better day.

E. T.

---

[1] Undated, but perhaps about January 12, 1914. Written on a postcard addressed to "Robert Frost Esq. / The Bungalow / Beaconsfield, / Buckinghamshire." The postmark is clearly legible and yet mysteriously corrupt, giving the date as "JA Є1 14."

3. Thomas to Frost[1]

13 Rusham Rd
Balham SW [2]

My dear Frost

I was nearly asking you to come here with me for the night &
when I got here my mother said she wished she had suggested it &
said also she would be glad if you would come back with me to-
morrow for supper & bed. I hope you will. My work may prevent
me from coming to lunch but I shall be at St George's at 4 & after.
I hope you will come there. If you can't do that but will come here
for the night, either meet me on the platform at Waterloo where I
shall be seeing my wife off by the 7.10 to Petersfield[3]; or else come
here direct, taking a train from Victoria to Wandsworth Common
station—this house 13 Rusham Rd. being 5 minutes off. I shall be
here by 8.

Yours ever
E. T.

---

[1] Undated. Perhaps about January 17, 1914.

[2] The home of Thomas's parents, just outside London.

[3] Where the Thomas family lived in Hampshire.

4. Thomas to Frost

at 11 Luxemburg Gardens
30 i 14   *Brook Green W.*[1]

My dear Frost,

Many thanks for your poem.[2] I have just finished it & liked it a good deal except the last line. I should like to know why you do not print it as dialogue with the speaker's names. Is it self denial & desire to cut off every chance of emphasis even by stage directions &c?

Are you to be in town next week? I shall be at St. George's on Tuesday at 4. But I might manage tea or lunch some other day if it suits you better—before Friday. I am here for another week or so before going into the country. I don't quite know where I shall go, but if you happen to know any really cheap lodgings in your part of the country will you tell me?

Yours
Edward Thomas.

---

[1] The London home of Clifford Bax.

[2] Probably "The Death of the Hired Man," which Frost had been circulating around this time (under the title, "Death of the Farm Hand").

5. Thomas to Frost[1]

Steep
19 ii 14   *Petersfield*[2]

My dear Frost

It could not be done. And I have accumulated a press of little things to be done before I begin & am flustered in the extreme. When I am next up in London I will let you know & we might have lunch together somewhere quiet. Also I will look at my map & consider the roads between us. But first I must see if I really can write something. I wish you were nearer so that we could see one another easily & our children.

Yours ever
Edward Thomas

---

[1] Written on a letter card addressed to "Robert Frost Esq / the Bungalow / Reynolds R^d / Beaconsfield."

[2] The Thomas residence from July 1913 until August 1916 (when they moved to High Beech, Essex).

6. Thomas to Frost

Steep

24 ii 14

My dear Frost

I usually write at once to make up for the invariable shortness of my letters. But this couldn't be instantaneous because I have really had some work to do. Today I rather think I began a fiction. I won't say positively.

The map doesn't discourage me. It is a day's ride.[1] I don't think more. When I am really into the book I will try it.

Many thanks for the photographs & 'Poetry'.[2] Your poem was really the only thing in 'Poetry' I was glad to read. I felt it missed some necessary vividness in avoiding mere 'poetry'. I hope I was wrong. I like the photographs. Some of them were almost a pleasant shock after what I imagined probable in your country (and here for that matter). I wish I knew that I would see that country. But you know already how I waver & on what wavering things I depend.

I wonder will any of your children like this book?

Yours ever
Edward Thomas

---

[1] I.e., to Beaconsfield, where the Frosts were living.

[2] Frost's poem "The Code," eventually published in *North of Boston*, appeared in *Poetry* for February 1914 (with the title, "The Code—Heroics").

7. Thomas to Frost

19 v 14

My dear Frost

I wish I could write a letter. But everyday I write a short Welsh sketch & a review. I read a bit & weed a bit & every evening type something, not to speak of touching the fiction still sporadically. And then there is the weather to enjoy or (here comes the laugh) to imagine how it should be enjoyed. Today I was out from 12 till sunset bicycling to the pine country by Ascot & back. But it all fleets & one cannot lock up at evening the cake one ate during the day. There must be a world where that is done. I hope you & I will meet in it. I hardly expect it of New Hampshire more than of old.[1] —I was glad Hudson turned out as I hoped he would. I understand those 3 approaches. If only you were to be in town & he too & he well & not afflicted by his sick wife & age coming on I would take you to see him. He is, if anything, more than his books. Don't get at me about my T. P. article,[2] which wasn't all that even I could do, but a series of extracts from an essay I shan't do. You could do one now. And you really should start doing a book on speech and literature, or you will find me mistaking your ideas for mine & doing it myself.[3] You can't prevent me from making use of them:

---

[1] I.e., Hampshire, the county in which Thomas lived.

[2] Probably "The Cuckoo," printed in *T. P.'s Weekly* for May 8.

[3] Referring to Frost's ideas about sentence sounds. Frost wrote to Sidney Cox in December 1914:

I do so daily & want to begin over again with them & wring all the necks of my rhetoric—the geese.[4] However, my 'Pater'[5] would show you I had got onto the scent already.

Your second note pleased me. I shall perhaps come soon. My wife & I are to have a week or so very probably early in July. We <u>have</u> to fit in several calls. If we can we will come to Ledington.[6] I assume there would be room (for 2 whole days).

Did Davies appear?[7] He had left town when I was there last. —I go up next about June 5.

Bronwen is suffering from flat feet & a stoop. She enjoys the new school[8] & the gymnastics. But we miss her. She won't be home till August. Now about August, could we <u>all</u> get into the Chandler's for a month & would they have us & at what price? The only difficulty would be a room for me to work in. For work I must. Will you consider? We shall try to let this cottage.

I don't hear when your book is coming.[9] I tried to get T. P. to let me write on it but they won't.

I wonder whether you can imagine me taking to verse. If you can I might get over the feeling that it is impossible—which at once obliges your good nature to say 'I can'. In any case I must have my 'writer's melancholy' though I can quite agree with you that I might spare some of it to the deficient. On the other hand even with reg-

---

"Thomas thinks he will write a book on what my definition of the sentence means for literary criticism. If I didn't drop into poetry every time I sat down to write I should be tempted to do a book on what it means for education" (*SLRF*, p. 140).

[4] Verlaine, "Art poétique" l. 21: "Prends l'éloquence et tords-lui son cou!" ("Take eloquence and wring his neck!")

[5] *Walter Pater: A Critical Study* (1913).

[6] The Frosts had moved from Beaconsfield to Ledington in early April.

[7] He had. See Frost's comic account of his appearance in a letter to Sidney Cox dated May 18, 1914 (*SLRF*, pp. 122–4).

[8] In Chiswick.

[9] *North of Boston* was published on May 15.

istered post, telegraph &c & all modern conveniences I doubt if I could transmit it.

I am pleased with myself for hitting on 'Mowing' & 'The Tuft of Flowers'.[10] For I forgot the names of those you meant me particularly to read, these I suppose being amongst them. You see that conceit consorts with writer's melancholy.

I go on writing something every day. Sometimes brief unrestrained impressions of things lately seen, like a drover with 6 newly shorn sheep in a line across a cool woody road on market morning & me looking back to envy him & him looking back at me for some reason which I cannot speculate on. Is this North of Bostonism?

Goodbye & I hope you are all well. Mervyn has been writing to Lesley I see. I hope he will go North of Boston before it is too late— North of Boston & west of me.

Yours ever
Edward Thomas.

---

[10] From *A Boy's Will* (published April 1913).

8. Thomas to Frost

Steep

6 vi 14

My dear Frost,

Let Lesley keep it certainly.[1] That is all there is to say really. I am so plagued with work, burning my candle at 3 ends. Every night late I read one of your poems. I enjoy them but if I did what I liked I wouldn't read them now. It is not fair at all. I just see how they <u>could</u> be enjoyed—which reminds me that I <u>did</u> enjoy 'The Generations of Men'.[2] Now for the same reason I can't come next week, not till about the 25th when we will both come. I have curtailed everything: am only just going up to Bottomley's to keep my promise <u>and</u> to work. So I shall be here until the 16th I expect. —Yes I quite see about using the 'naked tones', not the mere words, of certain profoundly characteristic instinctive rhythms. And No, you don't bore me. Only I feel a fraud in that I have unconsciously rather imitated your interest in the matter. —I didn't see the <u>Times</u> notice,[3] & am sorry for one thing to hear of it, because it shows the book is out, & yet I have not got it from anywhere. I kept badgering

---

[1] Probably the book mentioned in [6].

[2] Thomas apparently had a manuscript copy of this poem. It had been published in *North of Boston* on May 15, but it is clear from this letter that Thomas had not yet received a copy of the book.

[3] *North of Boston* was favorably reviewed in a brief, unsigned article on May 28, 1914 in *The Times Literary Supplement*, p. 263.

Adcock[4] for it. De la Mare might have done it in the Times—unless it was done in the column where books are acknowledged.

By the way unless the letter was sent to her in London Bronwen hasn't had a letter from Ledington.

I have dropped that fiction, so that's two truncated M.S.S. in a year.[5] I should feel vain at doing unprofitable things if I hadn't added up my earnings the other night. Something has got to happen. I keep saying, Why worry about a process that may terminate a kind of life which I keep saying couldn't be worse?

I will let you know later what day exactly we shall come. Oh, and £3.3 is satisfactory.[6] I will not say we shall come but I feel sure we shall.

Yours ever

E. T.

---

[4] Editor of *The Bookman*.

[5] The other being his planned book on *Ecstasy*, abandoned in September 1913.

[6] The proposed rent at the Chandlers' farm, where the Thomas family was to stay during their month-long visit in August.

9. Thomas to Frost
Wednesday [1]   _Steep_

My dear Frost,

I disregarded your letter. On Monday I had to go to town for one night & I had your book[2] most of the time in the train, 'Home Burial', 'The Housekeeper' for the second time. There is not a bad one among them, not one I haven't enjoyed very much—only the last line of each of those two leaves me with a shade of dissatisfaction. Which is a foolish thing for me to say without saying a great deal more. Pound's card is good.[3]

No I can't come this week. It will be about today fortnight that we both shall come. By the way, I rather think it won't be necessary to go down to Greenway. I should like my wife to meet Abercrombie, but there is not time for both, perhaps one without the other would be unseemly. We shall all have to go in to Coventry on the Saturday, unless it can be done on the Sunday morning.

I am assuming the Chandlers will have us.

By the way when I saw Bronwen yesterday she said she had received Irma's letter & had written two herself, but omitting Ledington from the address.

---

[1] Possibly July 1, 1914.

[2] _North of Boston._

[3] Pound had written to Frost, on a small note card dated June 1, "Your damfool publisher has not sent me review copies of your new book—nor has she sent one—so far as I know—to Hueffer" (printed in _TEY_, p. 451).

I wish you <u>would</u> kick some nonsense out of me. But I wonder if your kick is hard enough.

Now I've promised to make an anthology of Flower poems for a publisher who preferred it to an original essay on what not. Will you tell me of some? And I might just possibly be able to find room for 'A Tuft of Flowers' <u>if</u> you agreed & <u>if</u> I am not compelled to use a large leaven of <u>garden</u> poems—the book being mostly pictures of mostly garden flowers. Or 'A Late Walk' is more practicable in length, or 'Mowing'. But remember I have got to include, so to speak, Shakespeare & Jesus Christ.[4]

De la Mare, I gather (I saw him in town yesterday), had not seen the book, your book I mean.[5]

I hope you don't get the notion that because I say nothing about your book except what one could say about things one thought little of, therefore I am hedging. It is purely disinclination to sprawl about before your eyes as I feel I should do, more than usual, just now.

Yours ever
E. T.

---

[4] *The Flowers I Love*, with drawings by Katherine Cameron, was published in 1916. All three of the Frost poems Thomas mentions, all from *A Boy's Will*, were included.

[5] *North of Boston*. Thomas had suggested in [8] that the review in *The Times Literary Supplement* had perhaps been de la Mare's.

10. Thomas, "A New Poet," Review of *North of Boston, Daily News,* July 22, 1914

A New Poet

This is one of the most revolutionary books of modern times, but one of the quietest and least aggressive. It speaks, and it is poetry. It consists of fifteen poems, from fifty to three hundred lines long, depicting scenes from life, chiefly in the country, in New Hampshire. Two neighbor farmers go along the opposite sides of their boundary wall, mending it and speaking of walls and of boundaries. A husband and wife discuss an old vagabond farm servant who has come home to them, as it falls out, to die. Two travelers sit outside a deserted cottage, talking of those who once lived in it, talking until bees in the wall boards drive them away. A man who has lost his feet in a saw-mill talks with a friend, a child, and the lawyer comes from Boston about compensation. The poet himself describes the dreams of his eyes after a long day on a ladder picking apples, and the impression left on him by a neglected woodpile in the snow on an evening walk. All but these last two are dialogue mainly; nearly all are in blank verse.

These poems are revolutionary because they lack the exaggeration of rhetoric, and even at first sight appear to lack the poetic intensity of which rhetoric is an imitation. Their language is free from the poetical words and forms that are the chief material of secondary poets. The metre avoids not only the old-fashioned pomp and sweetness, but the later fashion also of discord and fuss. In fact, the medium is common speech and common decasyllables, and Mr

Frost is at no pains to exclude blank verse lines resembling those employed, I think, by Andrew Lang[1] in a leading article printed as prose. Yet almost all these poems are beautiful. They depend not at all on objects commonly admitted to be beautiful; neither have they merely a homely beauty, but are often grand, sometimes magical. Many, if not most, of the separate lines and separate sentences are plain and, in themselves, nothing. But they are bound together and made elements of beauty by a calm eagerness of emotion.

What the poet might have done, could he have permitted himself egoistic rhetoric, we have a glimpse of once or twice where one of his characters tastes a fanciful mood to the full: as where one of the men by the deserted cottage, who has been describing an old-style inhabitant, says:

> 'As I sit here, and often times, I wish
> I could be a monarch of a desert land
> I could devote and dedicate for ever
> To the truths we keep coming back and back to.
> So desert it would have to be, so walled
> By mountain ranges half in summer snow,
> No one would covet it or think it worth
> The pains of conquering to force change on.
> Scattered oases where men dwelt, but mostly
> Sand dunes held loosely in tamarisk
> Blown over and over themselves in idleness.
> Sand grains should sugar in the natal dew
> The babe born to the desert, the sand storm
> Retard mid-waste my cowering caravans—
>
> There are bees in this wall.' He struck the clapboards,
> Fierce heads looked out; small bodies pivoted.
> We rose to go. Sunset blazed on the windows.[2]

---

[1] Lang was a scholar, poet, and journalist with an impressive number of books on a great range of topics.

[2] "The Black Cottage," ll. 111–27.

This passage stands alone. But it is a solitary emotion also that gives him another which I feel obliged to quote in order to hint at the poetry elsewhere spread evenly over whole poems. It is the end of 'The Wood Pile':

> I thought that only
> Someone who lived in turning to fresh tasks
> Could so forget his handiwork on which
> He spent himself, the labour of his axe,
> And leave it there far from a useful fireplace
> To warm the frozen swamp as best it could
> With the slow smokeless burning of decay.

The more dramatic pieces have the same beauty in solution, the beauty of life seen by one in whom mystery and tenderness together just outstrip humour and curiosity. This beauty grows like grass over the whole, and blossoms with simple flowers which the reader gradually sets a greater and greater value on, in lines such as these about the dying labourer:

> She put out her hand
> Among the harp-like morning-glory strings
> Taut with the dew from the garden bed to eaves,
> As if she played unheard the tenderness
> That wrought on him beside her in the night.
> 'Warren,' she said, 'he has come home to die:
> You needn't be afraid he'll leave you this time.'

> 'Home,' he mocked gently.

> 'Yes, what else but home?
> It all depends on what you mean by home.
> Of course, he's nothing to us, any more
> Than was the hound that came a stranger to us
> Out of the woods, worn out upon the trail.'

'Home is the place where, when you have to go there,
They have to take you in.'

'I should have called it
Something you somehow haven't to deserve.'[3]

The book is not without failures. Mystery falls into obscurity. In some lines I cannot hit upon the required accents. But his successes, like 'The Death of the Hired Man', put Mr Frost above all other writers of verse in America. He will be accused of keeping monotonously at a low level, because his characters are quiet people, and he has chosen the unresisting medium of blank verse. I will only remark that he would lose far less than most modern writers by being printed as prose. If his work were so printed, it would have little in common with the kind of prose that runs to blank verse: in fact, it would turn out to be closer knit and more intimate than the finest prose is except in its finest passages. It is poetry because it is better than prose.

---

[3] "The Death of the Hired Man," ll. 106–20.

11. Thomas, "Robert Frost," Review of *North of Boston, The New Weekly*, August 8, 1914

Robert Frost

This is an original book which will raise the thrilling question, What is poetry? and will be read and re-read for pleasure as well as curiosity, even by those who decide that, at any rate, it is not poetry. At first sight, some will pronounce simply that anyone can write this kind of blank verse, with all its tame common words, straightforward constructions, and innumerable perfectly normal lines. Few that read it through will have been as much astonished by any American since Whitman. Mr Frost owes nothing to Whitman, though had Whitman not helped to sanctify plain labour and ordinary men, Mr Frost might have been different. The colloquialisms, the predominance of conversation (though not one out of fifteen pieces has been printed in dramatic style), and the phrase 'by your leave' (which is an excrescence), may hint at Browning. But I have not met a living poet with a less obvious and more complicated ancestry. Nor is there any brag or challenge about this.

Mr Frost has, in fact, gone back, as Whitman and as Wordsworth went back, through the paraphernalia of poetry into poetry again. With a confidence like genius, he has trusted his conviction that a man will not easily write better than he speaks when some matter has touched him deeply, and he has turned it over until he has no doubt what it means to him, when he has no purpose to serve beyond expressing it, when he has no audience to be bullied or flattered, when he is free, and speech takes one form and no other. Whatever discipline further was necessary, he has got from the use of the good old English medium of blank verse.

Mr Frost, the reader should be reminded, writes of what he or some country neighbour in New Hampshire has seen or done. Extraordinary things have not been sought for. There is but one death, one case of a man coming home to find the woman flown. There is a story of a doctor who has to share an inn bedroom with a stranger, and enters scared, and is at last terrified almost out of his wits, though the stranger is merely a talkative traveler offering him a hundred collars which he has grown out of. Two farmers talk as they repair the boundary wall between them. A husband and wife talk on the staircase about the child lying buried over there in sight of the house. An old woman discusses her daughter's running away from the man they kept house for. Here is no 'Lucy Gray', no 'Thorn', no 'Idiot Boy'. Yet it might be said that Mr Frost sometimes combines an effect resembling Wordsworth's, while he shows us directly less of his own feelings, and more of other people's, than Wordsworth did.

It is drama with a lyric intensity which often borders on magic. A line now and then can be quoted to prove Mr Frost capable of doing what other poets do, as in this description: 'Part of a moon was falling down the west, / Dragging the whole sky with it to the hills . . .',[1] or:

> 'There are bees in this wall.' He struck the clapboards,
> Fierce heads looked out; small bodies pivoted.
> We rose to go. Sunset blazed on the windows.[2]

or: 'Cottages in a row / Up to their shining eyes in snow.'[3]

---

[1] "The Death of the Hired Man," ll. 103–4.

[2] "The Black Cottage," ll. 125–7.

[3] "Good Hours," ll. 3–4.

The pieces without dialogue rise up more than once to passages like this about a deserted woodpile in the snow of a swamp:

> No runner tracks in this year's snow looped near it.
> And it was older sure than this year's cutting,
> Or even last year's or the year's before.
> The wood was grey and the bark warping off it,
> And the pile somewhat sunken. Clematis
> Had wound strings round and round it like a bundle.
> What held it though on one side was a tree
> Still growing, and on one a stake and prop,
> These latter about to fall. I thought that only
> Someone who lived in turning to fresh tasks
> Could so forget his handiwork on which
> He spent himself, the labour of his axe,
> And leave it there far from a useful fireplace
> To warm the frozen swamp as best it could
> With the slow smokeless burning of decay.[4]

But the effect of each poem is one and indivisible. You can hardly pick out a single line more than a single word. There are no show words or lines. The concentration has been upon the whole, not the parts. Decoration has been forgotten, perhaps for lack of the right kind of vanity and obsession.

In his first book, *A Boy's Will*, when he was still a comparatively isolated, egotistic poet, eagerly considering his own sensations more than what produced them, he did things far more easily quotable, and among them this piece, entitled 'Mowing':

> There was never a sound beside the wood but one,
> And that was my long scythe whispering to the ground.
> What was it it whispered? I knew not well myself;
> Perhaps it was something about the heat of the sun,

---

[4] "The Wood Pile," ll. 26–40.

> Something, perhaps, about the lack of sound—
> And that was why it whispered and did not speak.
> It was no dream of the gift of idle hours,
> Or easy gold at the hand of fay or elf:
> Anything more than the truth would have seemed too weak
> To the earnest love that laid the swale in rows,
> Not without feeble-pointed spikes of flowers
> (Pale orchises), and scared a bright green snake.
> The fact is the sweetest dream that labour knows.
> My long scythe whispered and left the hay to make.

Those last six lines do more to define Mr Frost than anything I can say. He never will have 'easy gold at the hand of fay or elf': he can make fact 'the sweetest dream'.

Naturally, then, when his writing crystallizes, it is often in a terse, plain phrase, such as the proverb, 'Good fences make good neighbors',[5] or 'Three foggy mornings and one rainy day / Will rot the best birch fence a man can build',[6] or 'From the time when one is sick to death, / One is alone, and he dies more alone',[7] or 'Pressed into service means pressed out of shape.'[8]

But even this kind of characteristic detail is very much less important than the main result, which is a richly homely thing beyond the grasp of any power except poetry. It is a beautiful achievement, and I think a unique one, as perfectly Mr Frost's own as his vocabulary, the ordinary English speech of a man accustomed to poetry and philosophy, more colloquial and idiomatic than the ordinary man dares to use even in a letter, almost entirely lacking the emphatic hackneyed forms of journalists and other rhetoricians, and possessing a kind of healthy, natural delicacy like Wordsworth's, or at least Shelley's, rather than that of Keats.

---

[5] "Mending Wall," l. 27.

[6] "Home Burial," ll. 92–3.

[7] "Home Burial," ll. 100–01.

[8] "The Self-Seeker," l. 149.

12. Thomas, "Poetry," Review of *North of Boston, The English Review,* August 1914

Poetry

This is a collection of dramatic narratives in verse. Some are almost entirely written in dialogue: in only three is the poet a chief character, telling a story, for the most part, in his own words. Thus he has got free from the habit of personal lyric as was, perhaps, foretold by his first book, *A Boy's Will.* Already there he had refused the 'glory of words' which is the modern poet's embarrassing heritage, yet succeeded in being plain though not mean, in reminding us of poetry without being 'poetical'. The new volume marks more than the beginning of an experiment like Wordsworth's, but with this difference, that Mr Frost knows the life of which he writes rather as Dorothy Wordsworth did. That is to say, he sympathizes where Wordsworth contemplates. The result is a unique type of eclogue, homely, racy, and touched by a spirit that might, under other circumstances, have made pure lyric on the one hand or drama on the other. Within the space of a hundred lines or so of blank verse it would be hard to compress more rural character and relevant scenery; impossible, perhaps, to do so with less sense of compression and more lightness, unity, and breadth. The language ranges from a never vulgar colloquialism to brief moments of heightened and intense simplicity. There are moments when the plain language and lack of violence make the unaffected verses look like prose, except that the sentences, if spoken aloud, are most felicitously true in rhythm to the emotion. Only at the end of the best pieces, such as 'The Death of the Hired Man', 'Home Burial', 'The Black Cottage' and 'The Wood Pile', do we realize that they are masterpieces of deep and mysterious tenderness.

13. Thomas to Frost

Steep

19 ix 14

My dear Frost,

Sew-and-sew is good.

Your letter came when my hands were full of a man full of platichewds, with whom I was bicycling off (on Thursday) for a night near the sea with James Guthrie an artist you've heard me speak of. I had a good ride there & back over the Downs & a swim too in a cold rough sea rather. But I am tired after it & have only been able to type & add a little rather dully to an article on the new moon of August 26 & you & me strolling about in the sun while our brave soldiers &c.[1] I doubt if I shall get nearer soldiering than I did then, chiefly for fear of leaving many tangles behind & not being able to make any new ones for perhaps a long time. So I probably shall see you before the year's old. I might go to Wales & to you on the way back. But I might just see if there is any paid work to do. I did my English review article[2] & have just corrected the proof. Your suggestion for others I scorn. Earning a living is a serious business.

---

[1] "This England," which appeared in *The Nation* for November 7. See [15]. England had declared war on Germany early in August.

[2] "Tipperary" appeared in *The English Review* in October.

We are losing Bronwen again this term. She got to London on Tuesday with her cousiness[3] who is here now. Mervyn for lack of anything better goes to school as usual probably. I don't think any of us will go to Ellis'. It is not convenient to leave this house & my papers &c. to the damps of winter & I don't want to be alone in it with only too free a course. I could go on with the autobiography but I mightn't. Is it worth while adding the little things that crop up from time to time which I have omitted? As it is an accumulation. Perhaps I ought to. Your opinion relieves me, even more. I hope you will lay your finger on anything that strikes you as incomplete or dubious.

I shall be glad if I hear Mrs Nutt has got a job for you & Mrs Gardner a cottage I can cycle or walk to this autumn & winter.[4] Next week or the week after I shall be in town & I suppose you may possibly be there too. But is Edinburgh off?[5]

Will you send Harriet something? The Spider on the war? or philoprogenitiveness &c. Kitchenet to please Mrs Gardner? I want to see her daughter, by the way.

There are some apples about here. So come if you can. And our damsons are still a sight both on the trees & in our biggest bowls. We have picked some blackberries, too. I wonder if you have ever seen the hop picking & smelt the kilns?

We had a man[6] here a couple of nights [ago] who has been living near Keene in New Hampshire, is returning there & wants to take Mervyn. He was a schoolmaster here but talks of blacksmithing

---

[3] Still in occasional use in the nineteenth century, according to the *OED*, "as a nonce-wd." for a "female cousin."

[4] This may be a joke on the strained relations between Frost and both of these women. But then there is some evidence of Frost's looking for work in London (and a cottage nearer to there) around this time. See *IMO*, pp. 252, 263.

[5] Frost visited J. C. Smith in Edinburgh for two weeks in October.

[6] Russell Scott.

out there & would like us to be at hand. Is Keene near any part you had thought of?

I've had a compliment from Australia on the Pursuit of Spring.[7] Otherwise I am as before and

Yours ever

E. T.

Our love to you all & I wish you were all within reach this side or the other side of the Downs.

---

[7] *In Pursuit of Spring* (1914).

14. Thomas to Frost

31 x 14

My dear Frost,

I would rather have had a bad ear than that letter. But now I have the bad ear too.[1] 'I cannot pipe to skies so dull & grey'.[2] I only hope that you wrote immediately after Gibson's call & in the worst pangs of it. When I wrote like that you replied that you wished I were near enough to be kicked. Well, I wish I were near enough to kick you, but have no faith in that kind of school. Did you want or expect a letter sooner? I should only have told you I was surprised to find you again like me, & I was inclined to write anything. But I find that when I write a moan people keep silent for a fortnight or so either because they think you will by then have forgotten or because they don't think it 'requires an answer'. It is no use telling you I could feel the same about a book (tho I don't know how it feels to have written 'North of Boston',) and with as little reasonable ground. I imagine that few written so early become assured of the understanding & admiration of such a variety of readers. But also I don't imagine that because a man has reasonable ground for some contentment at times therefore he ought to be content at times, though he probably will be.

---

[1] He had been suffering from an ear problem since early October.

[2] Charles Kingsley, "A Farewell," l. 2: "No lark could pipe in skies so dull and grey."

I didn't suspect all this wisdom when I began to write or I would have waited. What I really wrote for was to ask you to send me the MS of the Proverbs[3]

c/o Clifford Bax
1 Bishop's Avenue
East Finchley
London N.W.

I am to meet an artist there on Wednesday who wants to try illustrating them. But if you don't send it off on Tuesday or Wednesday address it to Steep.

I have now got the 4th volume (since September) of M.S. poems to read and pronounce on for fond unknown bards. Would this bring the warm blood to your cheek? In each case I have written hostile unanswered opinions without the least belief they are right or useful.

My only fun out of reading has been from Wilfrid Blunt's Collected Poems.[4] There is a man in them very easy to disengage. Do you know him?

I have just made myself almost ill with thinking hard for an hour,—going up to my study & sitting there,—that I ought to enlist next week in town. Now I am so weak I wouldn't show anything but my ear to any doctor. I am just going to do that.

I go on writing, unlike all the patriots, or rather as the patriots feel they oughtn't to.

What about the poems you wrote after we left? Send them if you feel inclined.

There is something wrong & artificial about this letter without more than one dot at a time. I am sorry. I shall be glad to have one from you with or without dots.

> Our love to you all
> Yours ever
> E.T.

---

[3] Published as *Four-and-Twenty Blackbirds* in 1915.

[4] Wilfrid Blunt's two-volume *Poetical Works* was published in London in 1914.

15. Thomas on England, *The Nation*, November 7, 1914

This England

It was a part of the country I had never known before, and I had no connections with it. Once only, during infancy, I had stayed here at a vicarage, and though I have been told things about it which it gives me, almost as if they were memories, a certain pleasure to recall, no genuine memory survives from the visit. All I can say is that the name, Hereford, had somehow won in my mind a very distinct meaning; it stood out among county names as the most delicately rustic of them all, with a touch of nobility given it long ago, I think, by Shakespeare's 'Harry of Hereford, Lancaster, and Derby.' But now I was here for the third time since the year began. In April here I had heard, among apple trees in flower, not the first cuckoo, but the first abundance of day-long-calling cuckoos; here, the first nightingale's song, though too far-off and intermittently, twitched away by the gusty night winds; here I found the earliest may-blossom which by May Day, while I still lingered, began to dapple the hedges thickly, and no rain fell, yet the land was sweet. Here I had the consummation of Midsummer, the weather radiant and fresh, yet hot and rainless, the white and the pink wild roses, the growing bracken, the last and the best of the songs, blackbird's, blackcap's. Now it was August, and again no rain fell for many days; the harvest was a good one, and after standing long in the sun it was gathered in and put up in ricks in the sun, to the contentment of men and rooks. All day the rooks in the wheat-fields were caw-ing a deep sweet caw, in alternating choirs or all together, almost like sheep bleating, contentedly, on until late evening. The sun shone, always warm, from skies sometimes cloudless, sometimes inscribed with a fine white scatter miles high, sometimes displaying the full pomp of white moving mountains, sometimes almost entirely shrouded in dull sulphurous threats, but vain ones.

Three meadows away lived a friend, and once or twice or three times a day I used to cross the meadows, the gate, and the two stiles. The first was a concave meadow, in April strewn with daffodils. There, day and night, pastured a bay colt and a black mare, thirty years old, but gay enough to have slipped away two years back and got herself made the mother of this 'stolen' foal. The path led across the middle of the meadow, through a gate, and alongside one of the hedges of the next, which sloped down rather steeply to the remnant of a brook, and was grazed by half a dozen cows. At the bottom a hedge followed the line of the brook and a stile took me through it, with a deep drop, to a plank and a puddle, and so to the last field, a rough one. This rose up as steeply and was the night's lodging of four cart horses. The path, having gradually approached a hedge on the left, went alongside it, under the horse-chestnut tree leaning out of it, and in sight of the house, until it reached the far hedge and the road. There, at another stile, the path ceased. The little house of whitened bricks and black timbers lay a few yards up the road, a vegetable garden in front with a weeping ash and a bay-tree, a walnut in a yard of cobbles and grass behind, a yew on the roadside, an orchard on the other.

How easy it was to spend a morning or afternoon in walking over to this house, stopping to talk to whoever was about for a few minutes, and then strolling with my friend, nearly regardless of footpaths, in a long loop, so as to end either at his house or my lodging. It was mostly orchard and grass, gently up and down, seldom steep for more than a few yards. Some of the meadows had a group or a line of elms; one an ash rising out of an islet of dense brambles; many had several great old apple or pear trees. The pears were small brown perry pears, as thick as haws, the apples chiefly cider apples, innumerable, rosy and uneatable, though once or twice we did pick up a wasp's remnant, with slightly greasy skin of palest yellow, that tasted delicious. There was one brook to cross, shallow and leaden, with high hollow bare banks. More than one meadow was trenched, apparently by a dried watercourse, showing flags, rushes, and a train of willows.

If talk dwindled in the traversing of a big field, the pause at the gate or stile braced it again. Often we prolonged the pause, whether we actually sat or not, and we talked—of flowers, childhood, Shakespeare, women, England, the war—or we looked at a far horizon, which some dip or gap occasionally disclosed. Again and again we saw, instead of solid things, dark or bright, never more than half a mile off, the complete broad dome of a high hill six miles distant, a beautiful hill itself, but especially seen thus, always unexpectedly, through gaps in this narrow country, as through a window. Moreover, we knew that from the summit, between the few old Scots firs and the young ones of the plantation, we could command the Severn and the Cotswolds on the one hand, and on the other the Wye, the Forest of Dean, the island hills of North Monmouthshire, dark and massive, the remote Black Mountains pale and cloud-like, far beyond them in Wales. Not that we often needed to escape from this narrow country, or that, if we did, we had to look so far. For example, the cloud and haze of a hot day would change all. As we sat on a gate, the elms in a near hedge grew sombre, though clear. Past them rose a field like a low pitched roof dotted over with black stooks of beans and the elms at the top of that rise looked black and ponderous. Those in farther hedges were dimmer and less heavy, some were as puffs of smoke, while just below the long straight ridge of the horizon, a mile or two away, the trees were no more than the shadows of smoke.

Lombardy poplars rose out from among the elms, near and far, in twos and threes, in longer or shorter lines, and at one point grouping themselves like the pinnacles of a cathedral. Most farm-houses in the neighborhood, and even pairs of cottages, possessed a couple or more. If we got astray we could steer by this or that high-perched cluster, in which, perhaps, one tree having lost a branch now on one side, now on the other, resembled a grass stalk with flowers alternating up it. When night came on, any farm-house group might be transmuted out of all knowledge, partly with the aid of its Lombardy poplars. There was also one tree without a house which looked magnificent at that hour. It stood alone, except for a much lesser tree, as it were, kneeling at its feet, on the long swooping curve of a great meadow against the sky; and when the curve and the two trees upon it were clear black under a pale sky and the first stars, they made a kind of naturally melodramatic 'C'est l'empereur' scene, such as must be as common as painters in a cypress country.

Whatever road or lane we took, once in every quarter of a mile we came to a farm-house. Only there by the two trees we tasted austere inhuman solitude as a luxury. Yet a man had planted the trees fifty or sixty years back. (Who was it, I wonder, set the fashion or distributed the seedlings?) It was really not less human a scene than that other one I liked at nightfall. Wildly dark clouds broke through the pallid sky above the elms, shadowy elms towering up ten times their diurnal height; and under the trees stood a thatched cottage, sending up a thin blue smoke against the foliage, and casting a faint light out from one square window and open door. It was cheerful and mysterious too. No man of any nation accustomed to houses but must have longed for his home at the sight, or have suffered for lacking one, or have dreamed that this was it.

Then one evening the new moon made a difference. It was the end of a wet day; at least, it had begun wet, had turned warm and muggy, and at last fine but still cloudy. The sky was banded with rough masses in the north-west, but the moon, a stout orange crescent, hung free of cloud near the horizon. At one stroke, I thought, like many other people, what things that same new moon sees eastward about the Meuse in France. Of those who could see it there, not blinded by smoke, pain, or excitement, how many saw it and heeded? I was deluged, in a second stroke, by another thought, or something that overpowered thought. All I can tell is, it seemed to me that either I had never loved England, or I had loved it foolishly, aesthetically, like a slave, not having realized that it was not mine unless I were willing and prepared to die rather than leave it as Belgian women and old men and children had left their country. Something I had omitted. Something, I felt, had to be done before I could look again composedly at English landscape, at the elms and poplars about the houses, at the purple-headed wood-betony with two pairs of dark leaves on a stiff stem, who stood sentinel among the grasses or bracken by hedge-side or wood's-edge. What he stood sentinel for I did not know, any more than what I had got to do.

16. Thomas to Frost

Steep

9 xi 14

My dear Frost,

The M.S. got to the right place at the right time; & the artist is already experimenting. I am very glad you still approve. I hope I shall soon be able to give you a printed copy to keep instead of that flimsy typescript. But my agent[1] isn't very sanguine. He has not tried America yet.[2]

Haines tells me you are embarked on Doughty, but perhaps on the wrong side unless chagrin leaves you very patient & kind. He writes to say Davies' new book[3] is all right. I hope it is, but had an idea it wasn't. I was going to send you a copy of 'The Cliffs'.[4] Tell me if it is worth while.

Now I am up to the eyebrows in article II[5] for Harrison & one on War Poetry for Monro. His quarterly[6] sinks to rest on its creator's

---

[1] C. F. Cazenove.

[2] I.e., to find an American publisher for *Four-and-Twenty Blackbirds*.

[3] Probably *Nature*, published in 1914.

[4] Charles M. Doughty's *The Cliffs* (1909).

[5] "It's a Long, Long Way," published in *The English Review* in December (the first article was "Tipperary," mentioned in [13]).

[6] *Poetry and Drama.*

breast after next number.[7] He isn't going to war, though. Did you hear that Hume[8] had gone? The only one of that sacred band. The rest stay at home for their country's good.

When does Abercrombie return?[9] I was wondering if Mervyn & I might come over in his Christmas holidays. But I might find it possible before. I did say the end of November. Now I doubt, because my wife is going to see her sister & Bronwen this week for a week & to avoid pigging it alone here I may go to town for that period & shall then not feel free again for a time. Cycling became more doubtful tho just now the roads are excellent.

This isn't a 1[d] worth[10] but I am hideously engaged.

Do you keep out mists? Cold you haven't had yet except what you harbour.

Our love to you all.
Yours ever
E. T.

De la Mare is ill with appendicitis & shortly having an operation for it.

---

[7] William Collins, "Ode, Written in the beginning of the Year 1746," ll. 1–2: "How sleep the Brave, who sink to Rest, / By all their Country's Wishes blest!"

[8] Probably a slip for Hulme.

[9] Since early September Frost and his family had been living in Abercrombie's house in Ryton, Gloucestershire (known as The Gallows), while the Abercrombies were traveling abroad.

[10] The price of postage.

17. Thomas to Frost[1]

Steep

15 xii 14

Dear Frost,

I am glad you spotted 'wing's light word'. I knew it was wrong & also that many would like it; also 'odd men'—a touch nearing facetiousness in it.[2] I've got rid of both now. But I am in it & no mistake. I have an idea I am full enough but that my bad habits and customs and duties of writing will make it rather easy to write when I've no business to. At the same time I find myself engrossed & conscious of a possible perfection as I never was in

---

[1] Along with this letter in the Dartmouth collection are typescripts of sixteen early poems, a transcription possibly in Thomas's hand of a poem from "The Times 1914," and an envelope addressed to Frost at Gloucestershire. The postmark reveals only the day of the month (the sixteenth), since the month and year were both impressed upon the postage stamp which has since come off. Not all of these poems could have been sent with this letter, since at least seven of them were not written until after the date the letter was composed, and at least one of them, "November Sky," must have been already in Frost's hands in order for Thomas to respond in this letter, as he does, to Frost's reaction to it. The sixteen poems (typescripts) found with the letter are (in the order I found them): "The Manor Farm," "The New Year," "The Source," "The Penny Whistle," "The Other," "Interval," "After Rain," "The Hollow Wood," "The Mountain Chapel," "Old Man," "November Sky," "March," "The Signpost," "An Old Song," "An Old Song II," and "Birds' Nests."

[2] Variant readings from an early version of Thomas's poem, "November Sky." See the poem in *CPET*.

prose. Also I'm very impatient of my prose, & of reviews & of review books. And yet I have been uncommonly cheerful mostly. I have been rather pleased with some of the pieces of course, but it's not wholly that. Still, I won't begin thanking you just yet, tho if you like I will put it down now that you are the only begetter right enough.[3]

I should like to see the man who was upset by you rhyming 'come' & 'dumb'. I should also like to write about you for the 'Forum'. But they wouldn't want me to, I feel quite sure. Only I will write to them just to see.

You speak of your 'few remaining weeks here.' But that doesn't mean any early move, does it whether you only leave Ryton or go back home. Scott sails tomorrow. He was willing to take Mervyn out & tutor him. He was to be learning blacksmithery & would teach Mervyn (if Mervyn would learn). But Mervyn hasn't gone, didn't much want to, while the proposal was a little too sudden tho I had the feeling it might be god's idea to get Mervyn away from me for ever that way.

Mervyn is to have Peter[4] for company this Christmas probably. We are expecting him instead of the Dutch boy[.]

My works come pouring in on you now. Tell me all you dare about them. I have been shy of blank verse tho (or because) I like it best. But the rhymes have dictated themselves decidedly except in one case.

I gather that Marsh is more or less engrossed now & reckoned not to be approachable, but I don't know whether to believe it. In town I saw de la Mare & that is what he said. But he & I have withdrawn from one another I fancy. At least I know I am never

---

[3] Shakespeare's sonnets, when first printed in 1609, were dedicated "To the onlie begetter of these insuing sonnets Mr. W. H."

[4] Peter Mrosowsky was an exchange student at nearby Bedales school and was boarding with the Thomases for the holidays.

myself so long as I am with him. Now I have put it to Monro that he might show 'North of Boston' to E. M.[5] We'll see.

I wish you were a day's walk away or were really at anchor.

Yours ever
E.T.

---

[5] Sir Edward Marsh was the editor of the series of *Georgian Poetry* anthologies. The prefaces he wrote for them were signed "E.M."

II. 1915

18. Frost to Thomas[1]

Dear Thomas

Nothing but business this time. It's what I'm full of.

I wish you would ask one or two kinds of people before I see you if they think the American Liners much to be preferred for safety to any other in this crisis. My own idea is that there would be no special danger in sailing by a White Star-Dominion Liner. We should save money and get put down nearer where we wanted to. I'd not give the matter two thoughts if it wasnt for the children. Just throw out a feeler where you happen to.

Did I say that our day would be somewhere near the twentieth of February?[2] If you wrote Tuesday you should certainly have an answer by that time but with not many days to spare. As I understand it your best way will be to let me speak for a berth for Merfyn now. You will have to put down a holding fee of two pounds and be prepared to lose it if Scott goes back on you. Authorise me to do it for you when I am in Gloucester seeing about our berths.

I have just stumbled onto a difficulty which, however, I think can be got over. If Merfyn were going with one of his parents he could be as young as he saw any object in being. Since he is sailing without either of them he should appear as sixteen years old in the manifest. So I am told. I dont know what there is in it. I will enquire further. You might see what you can find out by writing to

---

[1] Written about February 1 from The Gallows.

[2] They sailed, with Mervyn, on February 13.

the American Consulate in London. Say you are sending a son to— Scott in America to be educated. Say who you are and who I am that he is going with. Ask if he would better have a passport. Say he may be staying a matter of a year or two and leave it to the consul to mention ages if he likes to. Hurry this up.

Can you hold off your visit till Saturday? We are not sure to be at Ledington till Friday late.[3] Elinor is tired to begin with so I don't suppose we can hope to do our packing in less than several days. Let me know what train.

Great to see you again. There's a lot to say.

We had long talks with Miss Farjeon.[4] Seldom I have such a chance to expand. I should like to think I hadnt bored her with First Principles. —Oh and by the way let her know that Wilfrid has been here fondling me, but saying cruel things about Viola Meynell for having used my poem where it doesnt fit.[5] He happens to have her book for review. He will slate her. He spoke with peculiar animus that I had no right to understand yet thought I did understand. Bless it all.

Oh and one more thing. I figure it this way.

From Liverpool to Portland to Boston (second class)	11 £
From London to Liverpool	—
From Portland or Boston to Keene (direct)	12 s
Inci- and accidentals	! £

Yours ever
R.F.

---

[3] The Frosts had left most of their belongings at the house in Ledington while they stayed at Abercrombie's. Thomas's visit does not seem to have come off.

[4] Eleanor Farjeon spent a week with the Frosts between January 16 and 24, 1915. See *EF*, p. 113.

[5] Meynell had sought and received permission to quote Frost's "The Pasture" on the title page to her new novel, *Columbine*, and Thomas wrote to Farjeon on October 17 that Frost was pleased by her doing so. See *EF*, p. 100.

19. Frost to Thomas

Littleton, New Hampshire[1]
17 April 1915

Dear Edward

The goodness is in Lob. You are a poet or you are nothing. But you are not psychologist enough to know that no one not come at in just the right way will ever recognize you. <u>You</u> can't go to Garnett for yourself; <u>you</u> can't go to De la Mare. I told you and I keep telling you. But as long as your courage holds out you may as well go right ahead making a fool of yourself. All brave men are fools.

I like the first half of Lob best: it offers something more like action with the different people coming in and giving the tones of speech. But the long paragraph is a feat. I never saw anything like you for English.

What you say of Taber I shan't fail to pass along to his sister.[2] I am going to Stowe tomorrow at her invitation to see if I can find a farm there.

We are still unsettled. Hopes grow in every way but one. I should say we seem to have hopes of everything except more money. If some of these editors who profess to love me now had only loved me in

---

[1] The Frosts, back in America, were at this time renting rooms on a farm in Bethlehem, but receiving their mail through Littleton.

[2] While Frost was still in England Mrs. Henry Holt had sent him a copy of *Stowe Notes*, a book written by her brother, Robert Taber. Frost apparently left it with Thomas.

time to buy my poems when they were in MS.[3] It's not in me to take hold and write them anything to catch them in the mood.

I shall have Merfyn come to see us as soon as ever we know where we are. Scott bores me too, though I never got nearer him than talking on the telephone at 400 miles distance. I don't so much mind his messalliance as I do all his muddle headed compromises to avoid the single compromise of making it a marriage.[4] I had to laugh when his sister-in-law told me he was ready to make it a common-law marriage if she would come into the game to save Merfyn.[5] She was the lovely one—with a twinkle in her mind. But she wasnt messing up with Scott's troubles. And I couldn't blame her when I had seen and heard. Mind you, she's fond of Scott.

You must be wrong about your Christian Science Transcript. There is a C. S. Monitor and there is a Boston Transcript. I should like to see that review. I have thought (but I wouldnt say anything to you about it) that you might pick up some work over here as you come along up to us through Boston and New York. By all the signs there should be a few people in both places I could introduce you to. Thats more than I could have said three months ago.

Jolly to think of you at the Duke of Marlborough.[6] She that standeth in the shoes of the first Duchess is an American and if you

---

[3] Frost's contract with the offices of David Nutt gave over the rights to Frost's next three books after *A Boy's Will*. It included a clause which required that Frost have no direct dealings with publishers until after the fourth book, so as to prevent him from selling new manuscripts to magazines. During the war Mrs. Nutt apparently went mad and fled the country, never to be heard from again, which freed Frost from the restrictions.

[4] Russell Scott had left his wife and children for his wife's half-sister, with whom he was living in America.

[5] Mervyn had nearly been sent back to England by the immigration officials because he was not yet sixteen years old and was not accompanied by a parent or a guardian with ample means (Frost himself was near broke). But Scott's sister-in-law had connections in New York through which Mervyn was finally allowed to stay.

[6] Thomas had accepted a commission to write *The Life of the Duke of Marlborough* (published later that year).

pleased her might be able to introduce you to more people over here than I can.[7]

Will you have to visit the battlefields of Oudenarde Blenheim and Malplaquet?[8]

I have just had two letters from you at once. The mails continue to come safely through. I wonder when we shall get the first letter sunk.

Poor Haines will be sorry you couldnt get down to see him.

You ought not to be left out of this: I have had one note from Wilfrid in which he says Ellery Sedgwick writes that he had a pleasant talk with me on English traits[9] peculiarities idiocyncracies etc. Wilfrid wishes he could have heard that talk! I wish he could. It was all about Wilfrid's nice feeling for country society and the Albrights.[10] Amy Lowell says I have no sense of humor, but sometimes I manage to be funny without that gift of the few.[11] Not often, you know. Ellery Sedgwick (ed of the Atlantic) wanted to let it all out, but didn't quite dare.

Did I tell you Sedgwick said Wilfrid rather invited himself over here—asked Sedgwick outright if he couldn't arrange him a tour. That is not as I had it from Wilfrid. He was under the delusion that he had been urged to come over and save the country.

Looked at a little farm yesterday right forninst Lafayette.

---

[7] Playing on the title to Browning's "My Last Duchess." Lord Randolph Churchill, son of the seventh Duke of Marlborough and father of Winston Churchill, had married an American.

[8] The sites of three important battles led by the Duke of Marlborough during the War of the Spanish Succession.

[9] *English Traits*: the title of a group of essays by Emerson, an author important to Frost.

[10] The Albrights were a family of farmers who lived near The Gallows during Frost's time there.

[11] In her review of *North of Boston* (in *The New Republic* for February 20, 1915), Amy Lowell compared Frost's poems with the poetic prose of Alice Brown: "She too is a poet in her descriptions, she too has caught the desolation and 'dourness' of lonely New England farms, but unlike Mr. Frost she has a rare sense of humor, and that, too, is of New England, although no hint of it appears in *North of Boston*."

We are with the Lynches.[12] Old Lynch hates England but entertains no nonsense as to what would happen if Germany won. Every Yankee in America (practically) wants England to win—England and France. They all think you will win, but perhaps not this year. But few consider the war any affair of ours. No one goes into a war on general grounds of humanity. We extend our sympathy on general grounds of humanity. We fight only when our material interests are touched. Yours were when Belgium was invaded; ours weren't. Damn the Germans. Did I tell you of my friend Alice Brown the novelist who hung up a picture of the Kaiser in her barn and drove nails into the face like a damsel in Malory doing despite to a knights shield?

Well I have to run on. Let short and frequent letters be the rule.

Let me keep the poems. I suppose you want the woodsy letter from the parson. I believe I'll hold it over a while though to show Ellery Sedgwick. I would not have him run off with the idea that because I poked a little fun at Wilfrid I am no lover of the English—when they [are] right.

Yours ever
R. F.

---

[12] The Lynches lived on a farm in Bethlehem, New Hampshire, where the Frosts stayed as paying guests until early June, when they moved to their new farm in Franconia.

20. Thomas to Frost

22 iv 15   *Steep*

My dear Robert,

I have let more than a fortnight pass & now comes this from
Garnett which I hope will only please. The reason I haven't writ-
ten is Marlborough. I read about him all day now & must do for
some more weeks. And the reading is pap compared with what the
writing will be. It will all be undigested & useless inevitably. The
only good will be letting me deeper into the secret of how not to
write.

You might have spared your photograph. There might have been
a laugh in it, but nothing you need have feared. You can do better
with England than the interviewer did. But I don't wonder now
you are in no hurry to write your Southern journey or any prose,
tho you never knew what it was to write about Marlborough. Has
fame swallowed the farm or are you waiting to know how big a one
you can take now? There hasn't been a cow put in one of your let-
ters. You're a literary man like me. So you know I go on with verses
to the detriment of Marlborough: take the 2 best hours out of my
morning with I am afraid rather poetical things sometimes. Did
you think it might become a habit?

Davies was here a fortnight ago. You should have heard him on
Gibson. He explained the scratching by a curious vulgar error. 'He
has got a louse bag' a sort of permanent multiplying stud. He knows
because he found one in his bed. I should like to tell you what he
found in another bed which some other visitor or the host had

honoured—he was terribly ashamed* lest he should be thought the guilty: he will never go there again. We had really rather a good 2 days together tho I was anxious to be beginning my job.

I hope people aren't going to crowd to see you milking & find out whether your private life also is like a page from Theocritus. It will spoil the milk. You will simply have to prove that Amy Lowell was a damn right too discerning when she found you had no sense of humour & reduced you to——. Still, I shall not understand it if the book doesn't sell. What is the pirate doing? Will he hand over any of the swag?

I blush for your interviewer's portmanteau geography & chronology making you see the two great bards daily at Beaconsfield.

Well, I am a little ill, with the first chill I have had for years & it jellifies me. Next week I have to spend another week at the Museum. Goodbye, give my love to Elinor & the children. (By the way, have you a photograph of the children to spare, or will you have?)

Yours ever
Edward Thomas

*I give you 3 guesses.

21. Frost, "The Road Not Taken"[1]

The Road Not Taken

Two roads diverged in a yellow wood,
And sorry I could not travel both
And be one traveler, long I stood
And looked down one as far as I could
To where it bent in the undergrowth;

Then took the other, as just as fair,
And having perhaps the better claim,
Because it was grassy and wanted wear;
Though as for that the passing there
Had worn them really about the same,

And both that morning equally lay
In leaves no step had trodden black.
Oh, I kept the first for another day!
Yet knowing how way leads on to way,
I doubted if I should ever come back.

---

[1] An early version of this poem, with the title "Two Roads," was sent "late in April or very early in May 1915," in Frost's hand, to Thomas "as a letter, with nothing else in the envelope," (YOT, pp. 88, 544).

I shall be telling this with a sigh
Somewhere ages and ages hence:
Two roads diverged in a wood, and I—
I took the one less traveled by,
And that has made all the difference.

22. Thomas to Frost

Monday 3 v 15

My dear Robert,

I got a letter from you on Friday, the one I have been gladdest to yet, & not only because you said you liked Lob. I was glad to hear of your going off to Stowe 'tomorrow'. You are enjoying this period, but it is silly of me to tell you so. If you aren't you ought to be, because you are not writing about Marlborough. But we have one piece of luck. Two pairs of nightingales have come to us. One sings in our back hedge nearly all day & night. My only regret when I first heard it was that you hadn't stayed another Spring & heard it too. I hope the gods don't think I'm the sort of poet who will be content with a nightingale, though. You don't think they could have made that mistake do you? What does it mean? —I get quite annoyed with people complaining of the weather as soon as it greys a little. Am I really ripe for being all sound content, or what? 2nd piece of luck (still embryonic) is that Scott-James has some connection with an American literary journal called The Bellman & is recommending them things by me, beginning with a remark on Rupert Brooke. You heard perhaps that he died on April 23rd of sunstroke on the way to the Dardenelles? All the papers are full of his 'beauty' & an eloquent last sonnet beginning 'If I should die.' He was eloquent. Men never spoke ill of him.

But you have some poems by you fit to send out, haven't you? These editors mustn't go sour with waiting.

I find I can't write. Re-reading Rupert Brooke & putting a few things together about him[1] have rather messed me up & there's Marlborough behind & Marlborough before. I shall have to go up to London for the last time next week—for the last bout at the Museum, I mean. Bronwen is now at school again. I shall take Baba up & leave Helen to contrive some spring cleaning. I tell you—I should like another April week in Gloucestershire with you like that one last year. You are the only person I can be idle with. That's natural history, not eloquence. If you were there I might even break away from the Duke for 3 days, but it would be hard.

Are the children at school now? Or are you still 'neglecting' them? God bless them all. By the way, there was a beautiful return of sun yesterday after a misty moisty morning,[2] & everything smelt wet & warm & cuckoos called, & I found myself with nothing to say but 'God bless it'. I laughed a little as I came over the field, thinking about the 'it' in 'God bless it.'

Yours & Elinor's ever
Edward Thomas.

Don't send back that parson's letter and of course keep the poems. (I haven't quite stopped even yet.)

P.S. Here is Ellis very elderly & masterly about my verses, not finding one to say he likes, but seeing the 'elements of poetry'. The rhythm is too rough & not obvious enough. He wants to talk them over. I don't. Well, I feel sure I'm old enough not to know better, though I don't profess to know how good or bad it may be.

---

[1] Thomas's piece, "Rupert Brooke," appeared in *The English Review* for June 1915.

[2] Alluding to the old nursery rhyme beginning, "One misty moisty morning, / When cloudy was the weather . . ."

23. Thomas to Frost
Saturday 15 v   *London.*

My dear Robert

The Lusitania[1] seems to increase the distance between us, unless I am really suffering just from a week in London. This is the end of I hope my last week's reading for 'Marlborough'. Helen is at home Spring cleaning. I go back on Monday or Tuesday with Baba to begin writing. I have seen a few people at meals, Scott-James among others. He is English advisor to the Minneapolis 'Bellman', a pretty good weekly that may be persuaded by him to print me. The only news is that Hodgson is now in the anti-aircraft squadron, patrolling the East coast chiefly with special guns mounted on motor cars. He will be happier.

One of my reliefs in this week's work was to write these lines[2] founded on carrying up 50 bunts (short faggots of thin & thick brushwood mixed) & putting them against our hedge:

> There they stand, on their ends, the fifty bunts
> That once were underwood of hazel & ash
> In Jenny Pinks's Copse. Now by the hedge
> Close packed they make a thicket fancy alone
> Can creep through with the mouse & wren. Next Spring
> A blackbird or a robin will nest there,

---

[1] The British liner was torpedoed on May 7, 1915.

[2] An early version of "Fifty Faggots."

> Accustomed to them, thinking they will remain
> Whatever is for ever to a bird.
> This Spring it is too late:—the swifts are here:
> 'Twas a hot day for carrying them up.
> Better they will never warm me, though they must
> Light several winters' fires. Before they are done
> The war will have ended, many other things
> Have ended that I know not more about
> And care not less for than robin or wren.

Are they <u>north</u> of Boston only? I must try them on Bottomley. I sent him a small batch that didn't include 'Lob' & he put whatever may have been his feeling about them into a rather polite friendly form, concluding: 'My only real & serious criticism is that you tend to use words in the spirit of the prose-writer, respecting first their utility & the syntax which everyday use requires them to observe. When formal rhythm & metre are allowed to regulate the use of language, utilitarian purposes are abandoned; language is thus freed to move according to its own interior purposes of cadence or pattern or suggestion, . . . '. There is something in it; but nothing to learn. I can't <u>try</u> to write unlike a prose-writer or <u>try</u> to get freer from straightforward constructions. I am a little consoled too because what he liked most (& thought best) was a passage where I had allowed 'rain & wind' to come in 3 or 4 times or more usually at the end of a line, in about twice the number of blank verse lines.[3]

I have now gone the round of pretty well all the verse-writers I know. Ellis was kind enough to find mine 'eminently the stuff of which poetry is made' &c. Thinking he might make a book of them I did at last send a selection to Monro. He didn't like it. He muttered something about conception & execution as if they were different things. But I had requested him not to trouble to give reasons why he liked or didn't like them.

---

[3] Possibly "The Source," which is not, however, blank verse.

If you have a farm by now these remarks will easily sink into perspective. But I am thinned out by all this reading & smoking.

My love to you all.
Yours ever
Edward Thomas.

24. Thomas to Frost

Steep
Petersfield

23 v 15

My dear Robert,

Nothing from you for 2 weeks fully now. But we heard from Mervyn this morning that he had lately had a good letter from you. He is getting on very well now it seems. As I have written to him I haven't much left in my pen. For this pen has been at Marlborough for a week now at a great pace. It is better to be doing even this than wondering what will turn up. Not but what I have begun wondering though already—anticipating the end of this. So far I have virtually paraphrased from old books & my memory of others, & hardly any more, except some arguments about conduct & character. But it has been pleasant walking up & down, too.[1] Such a lovely May it is, hot & with a bristling wind. The nightingale already sings only in snatches at long intervals.

I heard from Abercrombie at last & he returned The Purple Land.[2] He reported that the baby had been ill & his wife worse but now on the mend. He said something about having wished I should come there, but I shouldn't. Wilfrid, I see had some dots in 'Poetry' recently under the title of 'Orchestra'.

It seemed I had dried up, owing to Marlborough, but I have done a thing today.[3] I shall send [it] if I find time to copy it. It came of

---

[1] I.e., to and from his hilltop study.

[2] By W. H. Hudson. Thomas had lent the book to Frost, who left it at Abercrombie's.

[3] "Sedge-Warblers."

a Sunday with no work but a cycle ride with Bronwen. It is devil-
ish like habit, but I am all rules & evasions.

I hope you have a dooryard as neat as ours is, with all the old man
& rosemary & lavender string & the vegetable rows fairly continu-
ous & parallel & the may thick in the hedges. Such sunlight we have,
& sleep through some hours of it & wake without surprise at it.

Monday [_May 24_]

Another fine day but a poor one for me. My mother was here &
I could only do half a day's work instead of what I had promised
myself, & I couldn't accept the situation, but shall have done by
the time this reaches you. Anyhow I will add the rhymes & any-
thing I can before the post tomorrow. Our love to you all.

Yours ever,
Edward Thomas.

P.S. Of course I keep thinking about the chances of coming over
this year. In any case it will be hard to seem to be able to afford it,
so that I could perhaps only risk it if I really made up my mind I
would see editors as much as possible. I dread them as much as that
keeper.[4] I hate meeting people I want to get something out of, per-
haps. —Well I've no business now to be writing a list of things &
people I fear. —However, as things accumulate (my mother's strong
objection to my going with things bad & doubtful as they are in
several ways seems to me not very reasonable but it tells) I don't
feel at all certain. Like everything else that means an unusual &
conscious step it looks impossible, like becoming a teacher or a
soldier—I suppose I ought to write a long short story about a man

---

[4] For an account of the incident alluded to here, see Leslie Lee Francis, _The Frost Family's
Adventure in Poetry: Sheer Morning Gladness at the Brim_ (1994), pp. 154–155.

who didn't enlist. I tell you I wish you were in Gloucestershire as God is ('as sure as God's in Gloucestershire' is a proverb you probably know) or instead of him. There are a good many moments when I feel there is hardly anybody that matters except God in Gloucestershire or any other county. I have been very impatient with people lately & yet sorry they have drifted off.

25. Thomas to Frost[1]

Steep
Petersfield

1 vi 15

My dear Robert,

A letter from you this evening[2] & after a very bad week for letters. I was glad. We both were. And we had a cheerful one from Mervyn on Saturday. Only one of his letters was complaining, & that was where he felt very much up against Scott. It didn't worry me; but Helen took notice of it to Scott, which I thought a mistake. Well, he will be very glad to change over to you if you do take that farm, & I hope you do. Are there any apples there? Send us a picture of it if you can. You know I like houses.

That review, too, was good, & the petulance at the beginning won't hurt you—or Hueffer, I expect.

I thought you might be getting near a farm by your missing a week or two.

I am in the thick of Marlborough now, 7 days a week at a great pace, but with very rare moments when I get something down that I wanted. However, the thing is to end it & perhaps get away for a few days, tho I do enjoy going up in the mornings & afternoons,

---

[1] Included with this letter in the Dartmouth collection is a typescript of Thomas's poem "Sedge-Warblers" (with no variants).

[2] Thomas mentions this letter to Eleanor Farjeon (June 3, 1915): "We had a cheerful letter again from Mervyn and one from Frost saying he is on the edge of taking a farm he likes with a mountain view. He is very brief and evidently engrossed but cheerful" (*EF*, p. 143).

sometimes passing the same tramp I overtook in the morning which makes him smile. I passed the same old man 3 times on the hill in 24 hours each time a little further up. I never saw a man move so slow. I thought he must be going to die & he smelt like it. But that was my greenness. When I came back the 4th journey he was gone, I suppose to Dicky Bram's at the White Horse.[3] The weather keeps wonderful & my landlord's bees up the hill swarm every other day when they don't twice a day.

All the talk now is of Zeppelin's coming to London. Everyone buys respirators against poison bombs & Helen worries. I can't worry in that way further than I can see, but one gets silent at times. They also say some kind of conscription is certain.

I am not vexing about Ellis's opinions. But of course I am practically shut up now. I send a few things recent & not so recent, & wonder if any are right. 50 faggots ought to be.

I shall be disappointed if Garnett's article[4] doesn't appear. It seemed to me it would get through. You got his letter, I hope. He was regretting I hadn't brought him to you; & you would regret it if you knew.

The nightingales must be hatching out. They only burst out briefly at intervals now, whether it blows or doesn't.

Our love to you all
Yours ever
Edward Thomas.

---

[3] A local inn.

[4] Garnett's article, "A New American Poet," appeared in *The Atlantic Monthly* for August.

26. Thomas to Frost

Steep
Petersfield

Sunday 13 vi 15

My dear Robert,

Your two letters came together Friday night. When I saw the Franconia postmark on the smaller I guessed it was the second— that you were there. I hope very much you still are & will be al- most as long as you would like. My next hope is that I shall see you there. But this is a funny world, as I think you said before I did. 'Rum job, painting', Turner used to say when Ruskin had poured out a can of words. I wish I hadn't to say more about poetry. I wished it on Friday night particularly as I had to spoil the effect of your letter by writing 1000 words about Rupert Brooke's posthu- mous book—not daring to say that those sonnets about him en- listing are probably not very personal but a nervous attempt to connect with himself the very widespread idea that self sacrifice is the highest self indulgence. You know. And I don't dispute it. Only I doubt if he knew it or would he have troubled to drag in the fact that enlisting cleared him of

All the little emptiness of love?[1]

Well, I daren't say so, not having enlisted or fought the keeper. But I ought to write about The Road not Taken. I ought to search for

---

[1] From Brooke's sonnet, "Peace," l. 8: "And all the little emptiness of love!"

the poem first among your letters. But I shan't yet. I am pretty tired.
I must own though that it wasn't a very honest remark that of mine.
For whether it was that I was deaf or that you didn't quite speak in
the verses I got the idea somewhat apart from the words. That is to
say I thought I did,—the fact being that I got the idea as much as
if I had skimmed the words, which I don't think I did. So at the
time I was content to deceive you by referring to the poem when it
was really to that idea not yet in the form of poetry which existed
in my head after reading. The word 'staggering' I expect did no more
than express (or conceal) the fact that the simple words and unem-
phatic rhythms were not such as I was accustomed to expect great
things, things I like, from. It staggered me to think that perhaps I
had always missed what made poetry poetry if it was here. I wanted
to think it was here. I don't know what an honest man would have
said under the circumstances. Well, I won't go about with a lan-
tern just yet,[2] though I am going to have a devil of a lot of leisure
which I shall do no better with. The Marlborough got practically
finished yesterday morning—26 days writing. I am going to cycle
for a few days probably up to Haines at Gloucestor (through
Swindon) & perhaps on to Coventry. And yet I hate spending the
money. We get scared now, with things 25% dearer than they were
& work so much more than 25% scarcer. I take no steps. I try to
imagine what I should do if I got to New York or Boston. For I
can't deceive myself into imagining I should be a new man. I know
I shouldn't meet any one nearly half way if I didn't feel something
of a friend in him & I know I should seldom feel that. Perhaps I
should not be much worse there than in London where if I want
work I can only ask for it uncomfortably or hang about without
asking for it as if I had forgotten what I came for, but it wasn't for
nothing. 10 years ago an editor having to say the first word said
'Well Mr Thomas what can I do for you?' and I could only say 'That

---

[2] Alluding to the anecdote about Diogenes the cynic, who went about by day with a lantern
looking for an honest man.

is what I came to see'. He laughed. It was almost clever in me then, but I can't <u>enfant prodigue</u> it now. So I pester my friends, or did when I had such. I suppose one does get help to some extent by being helpless, but when one doesn't—it is as if one had pride after all.

Still, I am thinking about America as my only chance (apart from Paradise). Tell me when would be the best time to begin. Are people back in town in September? I suppose I ought to take what introductions I can get. You will tell me if there is any way of living cheaply & yet not being in the wilderness. But what will your distance be from Boston & what the fare?

I am glad to hear about your 3rd edition. You must get something out of it. And then I want to hear that the Atlantic is hospitable. There is nothing in Garnett's article to turn your head. It is extraordinary only because it is sensible & goes straight to your substance & psychology. It surprises Sedgwick because he is used to seeing bards praised by a set of epithets & abstract substantives. It should be out in July I suppose.

Honest man (Marlborough used to think he was honest), I have found 'Two Roads'.[3] It is as I thought. Not then having begun to write I did not know that is how it would be done. It was just its newness, not like Shelley or de la Mare or anyone. I don't pretend not to have a regular road & footpath system as well as doing some trespassing. On looking at it again I complain only of a certain periphrastic looseness in 'the passing there had gone to them both about the same'.[4] Also I hope that so far [you] have not found that you had to sigh on realising it had made all the difference, though it had. You don't wish you had been Drinkwater. Another trifle—the lack of stops I believe put me off a little. There. If I say more I shall get into those nooks you think I like. It is all very well for you

---

[3] Early title for "The Road Not Taken."

[4] An early reading of ll. 9–10. Frost had already revised the lines for a reading he gave at Tufts College in May.

poets in a wood to say you choose, but you don't. If you do, ergo I am no poet. I didn't choose my sex yet I was simpler then. And so I can't 'leave off' going in after myself tho some day I may. I didn't know when I left you at Newent I was going to begin trying to write poetry. I had proved it was impossible. Have you got your lecture[5] written out or typed & can I see it? I am glad they asked you & got you to Boston.

I tell you those two letters were the best thing I have had since you were here. Odd, but they made me discontented too with what I knew I was going to do (& wasn't going to do) with the 2 or 3 days leisure I have now—the book near done & my youngest brother[6] here to keep me off it & fine weather to go about.

To think of your doubting Davies knew what shame was! I never knew anyone at all who so often got himself into positions that made him feel uncomfortable. Did I ever tell you that when he lived near us he used to carry home his groceries in the lining of his overcoat, & Helen asked him once what he would do if they began to leak out as he went down the street. He said he would let them lie & pretend not to notice. He would have been ashamed to be seen admitting (1) that he did his own shopping and (2) that he carried things in the lining of his overcoat. Of course you need not believe it. As to the bed, either a married couple had slept in it or a single man in distress. —He has just gone into his 4th London lodging already.

I read 'The road not taken' to Helen just now; she liked it entirely & agreed with me how naturally symbolical it was. You won't go exaggerate what I say about that one phrase.

This moment a letter from Haines telling me I am free to drop in on him next week as I hope to do. The weather keeps so fine though that each day it seems must be the last—just like last year.

---

[5] Frost addressed the Boston Authors' Club in May.

[6] Julian Thomas.

People are getting pretty black about the war, realising they have not got the Germans beaten yet. It is said however that we are really through the Dardenelles & the price of wheat is falling. It is said to be kept back to prevent rowdyism in the rejoicing.

Good luck to you at Franconia & all our loves to you six.

Yours ever
E Thomas

27. Thomas to Frost

15 vi 15
(I am really at my mother's house, having cycled up today)

My dear Robert

This is chiefly to tell you I have been re reading 'Mending Wall', 'The Hired Man', 'The Mountain', & 'The 100 Collars' & liking them—enjoying them—more than I ever did. Do you imagine this is to atone for what I said of 'Two Roads'? It may be, but I don't believe it is.

I have been talking to my mother about going to America. She does not really resist much, but pretends to assume I mean after the war. She does not really think the war will end soon, but does not want me to say it won't. I have not got much forward or I should not have mentioned it to you again now if it hadn't been that it occurs to me now how I should object to coming back after a few months, with no excuse left for staying except that I should like to. Remember that if I stayed away say 4 months I should very nearly have exhausted my savings besides having given the finishing stroke to my slight newspaper connections here. There is a weak alternative too—if some branch of the army will take me in spite of my weak foot[1]: I believe the Royal Garrison Artillery might. Frankly I do not want to go, but hardly a day passes without my thinking I should. With no call, the problem is endless.

---

[1] He had severely sprained his ankle in January, and it seems never to have healed fully.

It would mean Bronwen going to some very cheap school & my letting Mervyn slide rather, unless I had the boldness to have all my savings used up in one year & leave the rest to chance. It all comes of not believing. I will leave nothing to chance <u>knowingly</u>. But, there, I suppose the believers calculate to the best of their ability—it means stepping out alone with company when I should expect to remain alone, with neither faith nor forgetfulness but just a reluctant admission of necessity—[.] How much of it comes of unwillingness to confess I am unfit[.]

I finished the book—except for a touch or two that occur to me now in the ebb tide—yesterday morning & am renewing the slight dose of superannuation that follows such 4 or 5 month tasks. I have to look up a few things tomorrow at the British Museum: then a few more things in Seccombe's library at Camberley where I break my journey home on Thursday (this is Tuesday).

When I start cycling in Monday I shall have Berridge for company. Did I ever speak of him?—a chaplain at a lunatic asylum, who was a bank clerk before he turned parson at 35. He might have been the original of Torrance in The Happy go lucky Morgans,[2] but is much better—the saintliest, honestest, best-natured man imaginable, doesn't like everybody but thinks ill of nobody. A believer out & out, & thinks me 'perverse & pernicketty': tries awfully hard to like my verses—his ideal, when he was literary, being Plato-Rossetti, in which school he produced 2 volumes of verse: once wrote a sonnet (on a marble table in an A. B. C. Restaurant[3]) to the waitress who was most like a Madonna: has a son a Lieutenant in the East Lancashires: was a socialist before he turned Christian. We get intimate about once a year.

As I may not be able to write on my travels I will post this now, making two for your two.

---

[2] Thomas's novel, *The Happy-Go-Lucky Morgans* (1913).

[3] Aerated Bread Company, a chain of tea-shops in London at this time.

How are you beginning on the farm? Do you cut trees at this time of year? Tell me what you have time to.

Yours ever
Edward Thomas

28. Thomas to Frost

18 vi 15

My dear Robert,

These last few days I have been looking at 2 alternatives, trying to enlist or coming out to America. Helen points out that I could try America & then enlist if it failed, but not the other way round. Is it asking you to prophesy if I ask you to say what you think I might do in New York & Boston? You see I must not think of coming over to see you & cut down trees if I can't persuade myself there are definite chances of coming back with a connection or getting connections that would make it worth while staying for good or returning soon. Tell me what strikes you.

Nothing happened in town. I lunched with my agent who had had no luck with my proverbs & could only suggest an anthology of amiable things said in English about Russia, someone else having done something on these lines about France. Not me. I ran into de la Mare & I am afraid we gave one another hardish looks. Then I saw Davies who has got an idea that de la Mare is to be provided with a pension to eke out his £400 a year or so, & I confess to being sore at the thought of the dispensation.

I have now cycled home with some fine weather to my credit & railway fares saved: have added some touches to Marlborough & have only maps to look at before setting out on Sunday, Gloster way, if it still keeps fine.

If you can write soon.

Yours ever
Edward Thomas.

29. Frost to Thomas

Franconia N.H. U.S.A.[1]
June 26 1915

Dear Edward:

Methinks thou strikest too hard in so small a matter. A tap would have settled my poem. I wonder if it was because you were trying too much out of regard for me that you failed to see that the sigh was a mock sigh, hypo-critical for the fun of the thing. I dont suppose I was ever sorry for anything I ever did except by assumption to see how it would feel. I may have been sorry for having given a certain kind of people a chance at me: I have passionately regretted exposing myself.

Sedgwick has come over bag and baggage. He will print the poem along with two others in his August number.[2] I saw the proof of it a week or two ago. The line you object to has long since taken a different form. I suppose my little jest in this poem is too much between me and myself. I read it aloud before the Phi Beta Kappa of Tufts College and while I did my best to make it obvious by my manner that I was fooling, I doubt if I wasnt taken pretty seriously. Mea culpa.

I am doing this sick in bed—so to call the thing I am sleeping in till we know definitely where we are going to live. We came down here (from the Lynches) because our rent up there was running into

---

[1] Where the Frosts had their new farm. They had settled in by early June.

[2] "The Road Not Taken," "Birches," and "The Sound of Trees" were printed in *The Atlantic* for August 1915, along with Edward Garnett's article, "A New American Poet."

such money. And yet we have no certainty that this farm is going to be ours and so we dont dare to fetch our furniture from Plymouth.[3] There's a flaw in the owner's title as my guardian sees it. Damn the suspense.

You begin to talk as if you werent coming to America to farm. We have gone too far into the wilds for you or something. It was inconsiderate of us. But listen: this farm is intended for the lecture camp. We won't make it our winter home for more than a couple of years. It is a picturesque spot and it is in the region where I have to take refuge for two months a year from hay fever. That's all you can say for it. About all it raises is grass and trees. Some time we must have a real fruit farm again further down along. But this place will always be here for our lecture camp scheme when that shall come to anything. Meanwhile it represents a small investment: the year's interest on it is less than the rent we have been accustomed to pay for our two months stay in the mountains. I think the pine and spruce on the place will increase in value more than fifty dollars a year. I think I told you the farm is to cost $1,000.

You may be right in coming over in your literary capacity. Elinor is afraid the rawness of these back towns will be too much for you. You know I sort of like it. The postmaster asked Lesley yesterday "How's Robert?" He's a nice old nasal-organist who thinks God has given him the freedom of your heart and mind. I should say it wasn't fair to you to assume that you couldnt stand him. He might try to place you if you let him get acquainte[d.] And then if he should decide that you were intellectual (approximately) he would start marvelling to you every time he got a chance on the latest invention he has read of in The Scientific American.

He does[n]'t chew tobacco—he is a good Baptist—but many do here. And shoes arent shined. It is really the Hell of a country.

---

[3] The previous owner had agreed to sell the farm for $1,000, no money down, but tried, unsuccessfully, to raise the price after discovering in the newspapers that Frost was something of a celebrity.

The postmaster for instance traces his descent from someone named somewhere in 500 A.D.

I dont want to scare you, but I want to be honest and fair. The worst that could happen would be no worse than Fletcher that day in St George's. I saw Fletcher by the bye in Boston. Such a person to exist.

September would be all right—late in September when people are getting back to town. Bring all your introductions. Some of my new friends will be good to you. Some of them arent good to me even. That is to say they persist in liking me for the wrong reasons and in otherwise disregarding my wishes.

And there's nothing licit to drink here.

Other objections as I think of them.

As for the war, damn it! You are surely getting the worst of it. You are <u>not</u> through the Dardanelles and we know that you are not. Nothing will save you but Lloyd George and a good deal of him. You must quit slacking.

The Prussian hath said in his heart, Those fool Chesterton's.[4] I say so too. All the follies that England is like to die of are gathered together in the books of those brothers. And Belloc with his estimate of two thirds of the Germans dead and the rest buried is nothing to respect.

All our papers are your friends. But they all make hard work of your present predicament. I clip from the Boston Herald the most hopeful editorial I have seen lately.

The letter I enclose may amuse you.

We-all to you-all.

Yours ever
R

---

[4] Psalms 14.1, 53.1: "The fool hath said in his heart, There is no God."

30. Thomas to Frost

Monday 28 vi 15

My dear Robert

I have just come on here from Haines's by cycle. I had 3 days there cycling about & talking of you. One day at Gloster station we met the Abercrombies just off to London. He was very well & lively, but she is changed & looks done. We went to May Hill from another side but not to the crest or to any of the points we touched. I began to versify again but now I have had a smack in the face from the publishers of my Marlborough who say it is short of the stipulated length. Hodson[1] here promises to take Mervyn at his school for a year to prepare for going into engineering works in the town & I hope it will come off. He also indefinitely suggests me coming here as English master. But it is only temporary—while another man is at the front—and in any case I am not sure I ought to let it interfere with my idea of coming out to Boston & north of Boston, though if I could do it I should have broken some ice.

I've had extraordinary luck in weather, all fine days when I was riding, & this is the 8th day, & I began (as I thought) at the end of a very long period of dry heat. It is just like last year in fact.

Haines & I got on well enough, tho he is restless out of doors with his coffer for plants, his dislike of thunder (we had a storm), and his punctuality for meals. He doesn't fertilise. But he is a good

---

[1] C. F. Hodson lived in Coventry.

soul, & he only read one of his poems, a thing about a number of different flowers in the Lake District, incredibly undistinguished. I doubt if a botanist can write tolerably about flowers tho a sailor can about the sea.

De la Mare has got £100 a year now from the Civil List, & he was making £400 at least. I suppose his illness was the excuse. I was annoyed especially as I am told I have no chance myself as being too young & not as well known as many others who will be applying. Let me admit also that I felt they might have let me sign the petition as I have probably reviewed him more than anyone else. That is frank. The news spoilt one of my days' cycling. If he didn't give me such opulent dinners when I went there I should mind less.

I send you the rhymes I made at Haines's & on my way here yesterday.[2]

Helen sent me on Elinor's letter from Franconia & I was very glad to see it. You have had some luck. I wish I was there with you all.

Haines showed me a photograph of you. At first I wished I had one. But now I think I have a better one.

Yours ever
Edward Thomas

Out of us all
That make rhymes,
Will you choose
Sometimes—
As the winds use
A crack in a wall
Or a drain,
Their joy & their pain
To whistle through—
Choose me,
You English words?

---

[2] Early version of "Words."

You are light as dreams,
Tough as oak,
Precious as gold,
As poppies & corn:
Sweet as our birds
To the ear,
As the burnet rose
In Midsummer heat:
Strange & sweet
Equally,
And familiar,
To the eye
As the dearest faces
That a man knows,
And as lost homes are;
To the touch
As a man's old cloak:
But though older much
Than oldest yew,—
As our hills are, old,—
Worn new
Again & again;
Young as our streams
After rain:
And as dear
As the earth which you prove
That we love.

Make me content
With some sweetness
From Wales
With no nightingales
That have wings,—
From Wiltshire & Kent
And Herefordshire,

And the villages there,—
From the names, & the things
No less.

Let me sometimes dance
With you,
Or climb
Or stand perchance
In ecstasy,
Fixed & free
In a rhyme,
As poets do.

31. Thomas, "A Dream"[1]

A Dream

Over known fields with an old friend in dream
I walked, but came sudden to a strange stream.
Its dark waters were bursting out most bright
From a great mountain's heart into the light.
They ran a short course under the sun, then back
Into a pit they plunged, once more as black
As at their birth: and I stood thinking there
How white, had the day shone on them, they were,
Heaving and coiling. So by the roar and hiss
And by the mighty motion of the abyss
I was bemused, that I forgot my friend
And neither saw nor sought him till the end,
When I awoke from waters unto men
Saying: 'I shall be here some day again.'

---

[1] For this poem, composed on July 7–8, 1915, see Thomas's letter to Frost of July 22, 1915 [34]. I know of no evidence for this poem's having ever been sent to Frost.

32. Thomas to Frost

Sunday 11 vii 15

My dear Robert,

You have got me again over the Path not taken & no mistake. I can only plead that if you now speak the truth then I had good cause for being in two minds at the start. If only there weren't so many causes for not saying exactly what one thinks. And then comes the difficulty of saying it when one knows. But as to this can I doubt if you can get anybody to see the fun of the thing without showing them & advising them which kind of laugh they are to turn on. I am speaking of men in non-prohibition states. As a matter of fact I shall not mind no alcohol when I come to N.H.. I really think you like port better than I do any form of the creature.[1] But I suppose you are amusing yourself with imagining reasons for my (apparently) not wanting to come & live in N.H.. I don't expect to find anything elsewhere I should like as well. But I know I could not make any kind of a living on the land, & I cannot yet see that I should make more out of 'literature' than I should from Steep. When the camp school becomes clearer I shall feel differently. Last week I had screwed myself up to the point of believing I should come out to America & lecture if anyone wanted me to. But I have altered my mind. I am going to enlist on Wednesday if the doctor will pass me. I am aiming at the 'Artists Rifles', a territorial battal-

---

[1] OED *creature*: 1.d: "*humorous*. Intoxicating liquor; *esp.* whiskey."

ion, chiefly for training officers. So I must let them make an officer of me if they can. This is easier to do than to come out to you & see what turns up. But it will train me for the greater step. —I wish I could explain how it came about. But I don't quite know. Also a long explanation would be very superfluous if I got refused. I shall write again at the end of the week, as far as I can see. If I am rejected, then I shall still perhaps come out in September.

Thanks for the letter from Llewelyn[2] of the Chicago Evening Post. He sounds—I don't know his paper—as if he might do something. But tell me is there really anything I could write for your papers? I know some of them, like the Dial, are at least as good as anything we have got, but they don't pay well (I know) & they aren't in need of aliens. My descriptions—no. My verses—why should they, except to return the compliment? I have or had just begun to write again. I finished off Marlborough, the 10,000 words of deficit that I admitted, got to London & saw people & then home & a certain degree of peace. —My Proverbs have been accepted by Duckworths. They offer £10 as an advance. Imagine it. I wish I could get an American to do them, too. They are to have just a frontispiece. That is, if I take their £10 & have done with it. I am angling elsewhere meantime.

Oh, I saw Garnett in town. He was pleased with your letter. So was I. You & he should have met.

You won't mind this kind of scrap under the circumstances. I am clearing things up preparatory. What it will mean is a couple of months in England, a couple of months or more in France & then if I am fit, a commission: if not probably no more than guard duty at headquarters in France. So I am told. I don't believe everything I am told (except by you). The English camp is Richmond Park near London, which you may remember in my autobiography—where I fished & got herons' eggs. I shall be within reach of people when I have more than an hour or two to spare. Shall be! I

---

[2] Llewelyn Jones was literary editor of *The Chicago Evening Post*.

shan't <u>tell</u> them anything about my ankle. Well, if I—when I get over to you I may be all the more useful[.]

Mervyn likes it now. He is well & cheerful, so much so that he is very brief[.] By his photograph he is American.

I hope the next letter from you will tell me you are well & have the house safe & sound.

Yours & Elinor's
Edward Thomas

33. Thomas to Frost
Thursday. 14 vii 15

My dear Robert,

It is done. The doctor passed me yesterday & I am going up again on Monday to be attested & get my uniform. Seven of us were examined together, stripped & measured & made to hop round the room on each foot. I suppose I was too excited & he kept sounding my left side & asking if I had ever had rheumatic fever &c. There was one man of my age, the rest boys, mostly clerks. The corps is now only nominally reserved for the 'professional classes'. Now I am on my way home to clear things up a little & get a walk with Helen on the downs. —I hope this is not making you think I don't want to come out. When I do come I shall be readier to do other new things, such as lecturing, that is if I do not crock up.

Did I say anything about Merfyn's return? Helen thinks it had better be in December, to give him a longer period and a taste of the winter. I wish it could be with you, but you know what is possible.

I know more about tangents & indirection than I do.[1] I wish I had time to tell you about these last few days. If there is anything to forgive you would forgive me, I believe. But I don't feel inclined yet for explaining myself, though if you were here I should. Davies by the way looked serious when I told him & said 'Well, I suppose it will be compulsion very soon.' He thinks he thinks so.

Goodbye. Yours ever
Edward Thomas

---

[1] For *did*?

34. Thomas to Frost

13 Rusham Rd
Balham
London S W.

22. vii 15

My dear Robert,

Your letter of July 8 makes rather sore reading for me now, sitting in the king's uniform in the rain with a bad heel. That is how it began. Six hours drill & a heavy boot pressing on the big tendon. They say it is not hopeless. It is not my idea of pleasure, but I do want to go right through. My idea of pleasure would be getting in 'head first up to my ankles in (farm) filth & hard work.' But it was too pleasant. I really couldn't imagine it leading to a living. I would plough & hoe & reap & sow & be a farmer's boy, but without any certainty & not the smallest private means I couldn't set out as you did. It isn't in me. Of course I know I shouldn't starve & that that is all I can say of literary life here. I could not ask my father for anything. He has no more than he needs, tho it is true that he & my mother have more or less undertaken to look after my family if——[.] But try & forgive me everything by thinking what an asset I shall be in summer camp if I have been in the trenches as well as at Oxford.[1] I believe you know that to find myself living near you & not working for editors would be better than anything I ever did & better than I dare expect. There is no one to keep me here except my mother. She might come too. But I couldn't in this

---

[1] Thomas graduated from Lincoln College, Oxford, in 1900.

present mess pack up & get born again in New Hampshire[.] I couldn't have before I took the King's shilling.[2] Now of course I have to wait till the war's over.

But it is hopeless <u>writing</u> about these things, & I haven't <u>talked</u> about them since you went. I am hampered, too, by knowing that you have hardly heard yet that I thought of enlisting. Perhaps I ought to wait now till I have had a letter back after you heard that & not go on criss-crossing letters so.

A month or two [ago] I dreamt we were walking near Ledington but we lost one another in a strange place & I woke saying to my-self 'somehow someday I shall be here again' which I made the last line of some verses.[3]

I want to hear that you really have the farm, & that you like the school better than Elinor thought you would, or rather the children attending it.

We don't know yet whether Scott wants to keep Mervyn till December but if he does he will stay there (or with you) and return in time for Christmas here.

Yours ever
Edward Thomas.

---

[2] Proverbial for enlisting.

[3] "A Dream." See [31] above.

35. Thomas to Frost

27 vii 15

13 Rusham Rd
Balham
London S W.

My dear Robert

Another letter from you today making it all seem possible instead of that dirty expensive business of badgering New York & Boston. I let other people switch me off into a grand campaign which I disliked in all its details—that was why it seemed so grand. I was going to punish myself with (other people's idea of) virtue & what a married man ought to do &c &c. And still when you wrote, of course, you didn't know it was all off just because I took to khaki.

Before I forget it I am going to ask you if you can recommend my Proverbs to Holt (for example). Duckworth is publishing them this Autumn & has not arranged with anyone there to take sheets of his edition & says he doesn't mind me trying to get a simultaneous publisher over there. But if you would send me a word to say if you feel able to put it before Holt it would help, because if you can't Duck-worth can at once make his arrangements[.] I quite see that you may, however, not act for some good reason & also that it may be late for Holt to take it up. I wonder do you approve of the title of 'Four & Twenty Blackbirds'? I am hoping & believing this will not give you much trouble whichever you do. If you do nothing, keep the copy, which is a duplicate. If it will save time, make any terms you like so long as I have a royalty of 12½% or 15% rising to 20%. If they will advance me dollars, why, so much the better: but I don't insist.[1]

---

[1] This may be a fragment. 'Insist' comes at the end of the page, and there is no second page among the papers at Dartmouth.

36. Frost to Thomas

Franconia
31 July 1915

Dear Edward:

I am within a hair of being precisely as sorry and as glad as you are.

You are doing it for the self-same reason I shall hope to do it for if my time ever comes and I am brave enough, namely, because there seems nothing else for a man to do.

You have let me follow your thought in almost every twist and turn toward this conclusion. I know pretty well how far down you have gone and how far off sideways. And I think the better of you for it all. Only the very bravest could come to the sacrifice in this way. Davies is only human but he is a robber who cant forget stealing while his neighbor has anything left to steal.

I have never seen anything more exquisite than the pain you have made of it. You are a terror and I admire you. For what has a man locomotion if it isnt to take him into things he is between barely and not quite understanding.

I should have liked you anyway—no friend ever has to strive for my approval—but you may be sure I am not going to like you less for this.

All belief is one. And this proves you are a believer.

I cant think what you would ask my forgiveness for unless it were saying my poetry is better than it is. You are forgiven as I hope to be forgiven for the same fault. I have had to over state myself in the fight to get up. Some day I hope I can afford to lean back and deprecate as excessive the somewhat general praise I may have won for what I may have done.

Your last poem Aspens seems the loveliest of all. You must have a volume of poetry ready for when you come marching home.

I wonder if they are going to let you write to me as often as ever.

Affectionately R. F.

37. Thomas to Frost

9 viii 15

but Steep will
always (D. v.)
find me.

13 Rusham Rd
Balham
London S W

My dear Robert

I am a real soldier now, inoculated and all. My foot has come round & I am rather expecting to go right through my 3 or 4 months training & already wondering what regiment I shall get a commission in. It seems I am too old to get a commission for immediate foreign service. That is, at present. They are raising the age by degrees. As things are now I should spend at any rate some months with my regiment in England, perhaps even find myself in one only for home service. But I want to see what it is like out there. It has made a change. I have had 3 weeks of free evenings & haven't been able to get my one surviving review written. The training makes the body insist on real leisure. All I am left fit for is talk & cleaning my brass buttons & badge. Not much talk—either here or at the headquarters. The men are too young or the wrong kind, mostly. But I see Ellis, Davies & de la Mare & Freeman now & then. Also I have had 24 hours at home twice. I drill, clean rifles, wash out lavatories &c. Soon I shall be standing sentry in the street in my turn. In a fortnight I hope to be in camp at Epping Forest. I stand very nearly as straight as a lamp post & apparently get smaller every week in the waist & have to get new holes punched in my belt. The only time now I can think of verses is on sleepless nights, but I don't write them down. Say Thank you.

They are very well at home. Helen has Mrs Ellis with her for a time. Bronwen has holidays now & expects to be invited away. The cottage is to be let for September & the family to scatter a bit. Ledington & White leaved Oak seems purely paradisal, with Beauty of Bath apples Hesperidean lying with thunder dew on the warm ground. I am almost old enough not to make any moan of it.

You are not going to tell me I ought to have had the courage <u>not</u> to do this. Jack Collings Squire argues it requires more courage <u>not</u> to. It is strange how few people one knows at it. Edward Garnett has gone out with an ambulance corps to the Italian front. Masefield is doing something in connection with a hospital—the papers said he was working as an orderly—I heard he was organizing. Hulme (I understand) is actually out in or near the fighting line. 'Blast'[1] has executed a second number. Harrison continues to exhort and the 'Times' reissues the poems we didn't admit in August with illustrations. Do you hear of Chandler?

People get fined occasionally for speaking well of the Germans at private parties—under the Defence of the Realm Act.[2] I don't wonder. My father is so rampant in his cheery patriotism that I become pro German every evening. We can never so beat the Germans that they will cease to remember their victories. Pom-pom. I am sorry. The post interrupted this with a letter from Miss Farjeon who is distributing herself about the country—as usual. Nothing from you yet. I will keep this back till tomorrow in case. —But today has been too full & as I have a long march tomorrow I won't get up to remedy this but just send my love to you all.

Yours ever
Edward Thomas

---

[1] A journal edited by Wyndham Lewis. Its second number was also its last.

[2] Enacted August 1914.

38. Thomas to Frost
21 viii 15 *London*

My dear Robert,

The Arabic[1] had a letter to you in it written just after getting yours written after hearing about my enlisting. I don't think I had better try to write it again. Perhaps a letter from you to me has just gone down in the liner which they say was sunk yesterday, tho I don't know yet if it was outward or inward bound. I have just had a full morning's drill & so missed a train home & have an hour to slaughter. This is my 3rd full week of drill with my foot unhurt & nothing to complain of except 2 doses of anti-typhoid inoculation. I am still billeted with my father & mother, waiting for the announcement that we are going to camp. When I do go I don't know how much I shall be able to write. There will be some evening hours to spare but maybe no opportunity or real leisure. There may be a tent for reading & writing: I hope there will be. As a rule, however, even now, I don't want to do much when my drill is over. I have eaten my evening meal. I have still a review to write which I think never will be written. All I have done is an index to Marlborough and the proof of "Four & Twenty Blackbirds".

I am going to be homeless in September. The cottage is let, the children & Helen will be scattered. I shall spend my weekends with my father & mother. That is, when I am not on guard, which means

---

[1] The *SS Arabic* was torpedoed on August 19.

24 hours of duty & then 24 hours of leave; it always comes at short notice.

I like the life; I don't mind beginning my day with polishing buttons & badge & the brass of the belt. I quite like the physical drill which is very strenuous & includes running, jumping, leap-frog &c[.] But so far I can't talk much to the men I am with. They don't seek me more than I do them & I am a good deal alone in my minutes of ease. Close quarters in camp may help. I don't know at all how long I shall be there, but I understand that being over 33 I shall not go on to France at once but come back to London & take my commission there if one is offered. I shall then probably have another period of some months training before I am sent wherever I am sent. The tendency at present, I hear, is to keep older fresh officers at home. But one knows nothing & one ceases to be curious; I don't really look forward more than a week, except for a moment perhaps now & then when I am doing extended order drill exactly as if under fire on the battlefield, & more briefly still when the eyes <u>nearly</u> water as we march with or without a band.

I hear that Hulme has been slightly wounded & is back in his old haunts. Garnett is about to leave for the Italian front in an ambulance section. Monro is in the country with his girl. Haines says he would go mad if he enlisted but I don't know what he means except that he has a queer eye. Now I must get off to my train.

Monday [August 23]

I had my 24 hours at home & all fine. At last we could picnic, Helen, Baba & I. I put in some turnip seeds & pulled up some weeds & took away more underclothes for camp & then it was all over. Helen & Baba go to the seaside on Thursday for a week, then to London for a little while & I <u>may</u> still be here. Helen is waiting for a good opportunity to write again to Elinor. Two letters from her must have gone astray. <u>One</u> I addressed for her when I was with

Haines at Gloster in July. She has been very busy with an extra child to look after & sometimes Mrs Ellis or Mrs Ransome. And she may be more anxious about things than she says. I know she felt very black about recent events. But with the big Russian naval victory & the British fleet in the Baltic she may feel better today.

I wish you had really got your farm. When you write anything send it please, if you don't feel I am unfit for reading; all I have read since I joined is "Cymbeline" again. I find I read it every year now & find it new & better. I look forward to reading it in peace. Another anniversary.[2] You have given me several. I remember you for instance by the ripening of the Astrakhan apples in my father's garden. You must give me some more & share some.

Yours ever with my love to you all
Edward Thomas
13 Rusham Rd
Balham
London SW

28th

I have some time on my hands at Headquarters today & have a pile of 1000 blankets in an empty drill hall to recline in. So far it is very dull defending ones wives & mothers & sisters & daughters from the Germans. I live with my people & spend 6 or 7 hours a day here or drilling in Regents Park. This weekend I hope to have 24 hours at home. It is decidedly a holiday except that I have Marlborough proofs to correct. By the way I only cleared a little over £40 by writing the Marlborough. Of course you are quite right in doubting whether it would have been my last commission, but not if you think I was mistaken about the extent to which my earning in general was declining. My country had virtually deserted me before I decided not to desert it.

---

[2] Referring to the holiday at Ledington of the previous August.

So far I am an indigested lump in this battalion. The men I am up against are mostly clerks of some sort with intelligent newspaper opinions and an interest in their clothes & in keeping up the social standing of the corps. Our motto is Cum Marte Minerva. Lord Leighton was one of the founders & originally the majority of the men were public school and professional or literary men & the like. But they let in anybody now who will pay 25/- a year subscription. They don't quite understand what I say except when I say Yes or No. The great majority are under 25. —It is a question now whether I should have been worse off say in the Welch Fusiliers with a mixture of clerks & shopmen & manual workers. Perhaps I allowed myself too easily to be persuaded I could not have stood their ways. For though I am admittedly a superior person[3] I am not as particular as some people. Well, I daresay any one 100 men are about the same as any other 100.

I enjoyed Richard Burton's letter. I like those people who understand so well how timorous others are. Till I got to his signature I thought he was a she.

Your letter wasn't more inconclusive than was just. It is useless to tell you now that it would have put me right off the plan that Garnett & others were letting me in for.[4] They see me as a rather helpless person who needs to make money for a family & I let them go on seeing me so. Yet I knew right away that for me to act as if I were a smart literary bloke & get my coming advertised as such would be rather worse than being such in fact, & I should have penalised my real self heavily by trying to live up [to] it. As a matter of fact I shouldn't have tried, but should just have let in my backers. I know.

Nobody persuaded me into this, not even myself.

Yours ever
Edward Thomas

---

[3] As an Oxford graduate, Thomas would have known the limerick about statesman and Oxford graduate George Curzon: "My name is George Nathaniel Curzon, / I am a most superior person. / My cheek is pink, / My hair is sleek, / I dine at Blenheim once a week."

[4] Garnett had hoped to get Thomas a position in a propaganda lecture-tour.

39. Thomas to Frost

Friday 3 ix 15

13 Rusham Rd. Balham,
London SW.

My dear Robert

I have again got some free time. At last I have been put on guard which means being at headquarters 24 hours on end with 2 hours on & two hours off duty (but on the spot), the duty being partly sentry outside & partly running messages for officers inside. Even in the middle of the night each of the six is called up in order for an hour to clean up some part of the building. Then we get 24 hours leave after the guard is changed. We are all now (except the 3 on duty), 3 of us & a corporal in charge, killing time before supper. We gossip a little at a distance, the corporal leading, being an old soldier, who fought in the Boer War, & was a cavalry captain in this war till the expense of living broke him & he joined this corps to train for an infantry commission. He talks about women, & the rest try not to show what they know or don't know on the subject. The 2 others are a schoolmaster from the west & a schoolboy who ought to have been at Oxford now, a very serious boy reading 'the food of the Gods'[1] at this moment.

We are still not promised camp at all soon. I have begun musketry. I have lectures on making maps. Once a week we have night operations to get us used to the sound & sight of troops in the dark. Once a week we have a march round Hampstead ending with a

---

[1] H. G. Wells, *The Food of the Gods, and How it Came to Earth.*

swim. It is all like being somebody else, or like being in a dream of school. The latest gossip is that this regiment has to provide 250 officers a month, & as there are about 1000 in the foreign service battalion which I am in, I may find myself with a commission within 3 months. In one day at the Dardanelles 130 officers were lost. And they say the thing is a failure & only prolonged because it is not easy to draw back. It is also said that in France they expect the end in October.

It is amusing to watch the corporal take decidedly the larger half of a piece of butter that has to do for two—and toss a penny well away from you when it is a question which is to pay for something. But of course this sort of thing can be learnt outside South Africa. Amusing too to hear him pronounce that though he is broad-minded he dislikes the works of Victoria Cross.

I was lured into sending some of my poems for Bottomley to let Abercrombie see—he having already shown Abercrombie my 'English Words'[2] without my consent. Haines has just told me Abercrombie likes them a good deal. I wonder. Do you know—at the last moment the Oxford Press asked me to fill up 2 pages that were blank in my anthology[3] & I put in 60 lines of my own over my pseudonym.[4] But now I can't think of writing. The country is a little strange to me. It seems as if in my world there was no Autumn though they are just picking hops in Kent. On Hampstead Heath the other day I watched the bees at the bramble flowers & green blackberries & they looked so unfamiliar & with a kind of ugliness, partly but not wholly due to the fact that the earth around about was dirty London earth. I won't make more of it than it is though.

---

[2] Probably an early title for "Words."

[3] *This England: An Anthology from Her Writers.*

[4] "Haymaking," and "The Manor Farm" appeared under the name Edward Eastaway.

Sunday [*September 5*]

As it happened I had 2 hours sleeplessness the night I was on guard after writing this & made it tolerable by making blank verses suggested by what I had just written to you. I had to. But I couldn't finish them & now they are practically gone.

Helen Bronwen & Baba are all collected here again at my mother's. It is a London Sunday, & the loveliest warm bright weather after a cold bright hazy morning that ever was in September. Bronwen & I have just walked 4 or 5 miles of streets & crowds. I stand it better with her but it is pretty bad—all the mean or villa streets that have filled the semi-rural places I knew 25 years ago. It is tiring. Perhaps I won't write anymore this time—but by the way Haines mentioned in his last letter that Abercrombie had written to you & supposed you hadn't got the letter. Haines considers 'Franconia' vague as an address. I must remember to tell him it isn't.

I saw Hudson this evening (Monday). We got talking of you because he had seen Howells on the subject.[5] He is very tired of Gibson's poetry.

By the way, I have heard that Hueffer is now a lieutenant.

Goodbye. I still hope there may be a letter from you this time. My love to you all. Helen & Baba have gone away to the John Freemans or they would send theirs.

Yours ever
Edward Thomas

P.S. Of course <u>Steep</u> always finds me so long as I am in this world.

---

[5] William Dean Howells favorably reviewed *North of Boston* in *Harpers* for September.

40. Thomas to Frost

Monday about Oct. 3.[2]   *High Beech*[1]

(but don't address me here. Steep is always best)

My dear Robert,

A letter from you again at last. It was more welcome than you
might imagine if you saw how dismal I am for no intelligible rea-
son. We have just had 2 beautiful sunny days & the oaks & beeches
of the forest don't look autumnal yet. But perhaps it is the autumn
& the crowd & the discomfort & the solitude. I have made one or
two acquaintance,[3] but it is still solitude. Nobody seeks me out &
I am too something to seek out those I want. Well, I won't talk
about these things that will be so different when you get the let-
ter & so unimaginable in Franconia. Mervyn likes Franconia,
down to the look of the houses there. I quite agree with you about
the difference between America & East Alstead, but as it isn't easy
& might be expensive to remedy it in the few months left per-
haps he had better return to Scott at the end of the month with
you. It is hard to feel as sure as you do that the war will end soon,
so I must be as careful as I can. In any case I think Mervyn should
get home in December by an American ship & go to Hodson's

---

[1] Thomas arrived at camp at High Beech about the end of September.

[2] Monday would have been October 4th.

[3] According to the OED (3.A), *acquaintance* can still be plural (as in Burns' "Should auld
acquaintance be forgot . . .").

school in Coventry & then within a year to an engineering works there.

There is a devil of a crowd in the canteen tonight & I go to the trouble of disliking angrily quite a number of men at sight. So many things have to be done here besides learning to be an officer. And by the way we have just been temporarily diverted into quite un-military work—digging drains, carpentering &c which makes me impatient. Well, also, I am looking forward to being at Steep again for a day at the end of the week, & it annoys me to think a foxhunting major can prevent me if he happens not to be in a good temper—a man like a mandrill, though he may not have a blue behind.

The next best thing to having you here is having the space (not a void) that nobody else can fill. Don't you worry to say anything about me. If I did anything it was as easy as keeping alive, easier & much pleasanter. The objection to Garnett[4] must be that it reminds people you were over here & gives you a shade too much of English in your composition; for the moment—more English than I feel in this room full of the cockney accent. The officers even are almost all cockneys. The article makes you seem as superior a person as I am here.

Now it is nearing call over & I shall get my bed ready.

No need for you to explain how it is you can't have Mervyn in the house longer. I quite understand. I am only very sorry Elinor is not as fit as usual & hope she will have a happier turn before long.[5] You don't say if the farm, apart from the house, goes well & is really yours.

—I wish I knew <u>what</u> it would cost for Mervyn to lodge near you & go to school just till December. If it is very little more than it costs for him to stay at Alstead he certainly should do it, that is

---

[4] I.e., to Garnett's article in *The Atlantic*.

[5] Elinor was in the midst of a difficult pregnancy.

provided it doesn't mean much addition to your work & trouble in the house. I leave it to you to decide on this.

Tuesday [*October 5*]

I meant this to be longer, but today 2 of us are digging clay & spading it into a cart, with a bully over us, & it is too tiring. They have just gone to unload the cart & I have a few minutes to spare in the forest, but I am not equal to more than trying to rest. It seems foolish to give men such jobs who are going to be officers in a few weeks. We may have a fortnight or even more of them. —One of my brothers[6] has just joined this regiment, but I expect to be away from here before he arrives. I shan't be sorry to go if it means getting a commission soon after. Men seem to think that any great move of the Allies will take all of us to Flanders pretty soon now. Apparently any man who will stand up & get shot is useful however hurried his training.

Goodbye. My love to Mervyn & all of you.

P.T.O. Edward Thomas

P.S. You haven't yet mentioned the M.S. of my 'Four & Twenty Blackbirds' which I sent you 2 months or so ago. I only speak of it in case they never reached you, though they were registered. If they haven't, there is nothing to say except that Duckworth is publishing them soon. I sent them in case you could suggest them to an American for simultaneous publication over there. My 'Keats', my 'Marlborough' & the anthology are all to appear with the Proverbs or about the same time.[7]

---

[6] Reggie Thomas.

[7] *Keats* (1916), *The Life of the Duke of Marlborough* (1915), *This England* (1915), *Four-and-Twenty Blackbirds* (1915).

41. Thomas to Frost

Tuesday   *High Beech.*
12.x.15.

My dear Robert

Two letters from you came soon after I posted my last—the two in which you spoke of Mervyn. We were very glad at what you said of him, Helen & I—for I was at home just for the Saturday night last week—though I wasn't quite so wholly happy about it because I believe I planted that frightened expression in Mervyn's face: perhaps I told you before; but if not I won't go into it now. Scott certainly didn't do it. What you say makes me feel sure now that it has done Mervyn good. I wish he could have another long turn with you. Helen was willing for him to stay after December, but I might well be going out to France soon after Christmas & I should like to see him first.

Anything you can do for 'Four & Twenty Blackbirds' I shall be pleased by. If you can't do anything I shall not worry at all, or be disappointed. There was very little time nor was I at all sure you would feel you could attempt anything. As a matter of fact I expect Duckworth will publish the book this month.

I don't write now. Perhaps I should if I had an interval as I did when my foot was bad. (It gives me no trouble now except to put on a slight bandage daily.) But while this work is on I find it hard to do many things I used to do. The compensation is that I neither read nor want to read. Many of the men round me read quite a lot of military things & the newspapers & some fiction. I practically never look at print. If I could it would solve the difficulty of the long cold evenings. When I do write again I shall send it on to you. I believe I sent you most of the last things—'Aspens', 'Cock-crow' &c. Abercrombie hasn't said anything directly. By the way I think I mentioned he had got some kind of a grant recently. Probably Haines has if I haven't.

I stopped this on Monday night because we had a lecture on Discipline, Duty &c from the Colonel. Such a lot of ordinary brutal morality masquerading as something very un-German & gentlemanly &c. Then last night there was bayonet fighting to watch & some night operation—merely movements executed in silence, with command whispered down the ranks, in very black darkness. So I have missed a post. And today I am pretty tired after a lot of marching in beautiful very warm still weather. We have had another fortnight of fine weather & hardly any rain; at home it was very pleasant. Maitland Radford was there by the way. He is resting for a month or 2 to recover from his year's doctoring in France. Eleanor Farjeon too was there. But I got there late Friday night & had to leave early Sunday morning, & only had time to plant some cabbages & go up to the study & light a fire there. I picked about 10 pounds of apples off our little trees & some great pears. I hope you have some as good, so that you eat them till your teeth are sad with them.

The air here is full of rumours. Some say we are all going to leave the camp in a week to make way for 300 young officers. There is a remote chance that they may try to turn me into an instructor of some kind. I am rather loth to entertain the idea, partly because now I have taken the step the only way to satisfy my vanity is to become an officer & go out.

Now I have got to hurry away. It has been a week of busy evenings with no spare time.

With love to all of you
Ever yours
Edward Thomas

42. Thomas to Frost

Saturday　　　　　*Steep, Petersfield*[1]

6 xi 15

My dear Robert,

I am up in my study for half an hour to light a fire to keep the books dry: I am leaving the cobwebs & the dust & writing to you instead. I am home on leave just for 2 days,—strictly speaking, <u>without</u> leave, & I shan't know what will come of it till Monday is got through. However, by the time you get this I expect I shall have recovered even if I am found out. The point is I have no duties till Monday. <u>But</u> there is a rumour we may suddenly all be called up & sent somewhere (or home again), just to see that we come when called & come quickly & equipped. Some careful officers refused their men leave to go out of town in case. But I had an excuse for taking the risk because I am for the time being in an anomalous position, belonging to one Company, but attached to another & engaged in instructing (under an officer) in mapreading &c. I am Lance-corporal now, instead of private. This means a school-masterish life. I (and several others) help the men during lectures, explaining, doing their problems for them &c, & sometimes taking them out on Hampstead Heath & showing them how to sketch a map with the help of the prismatic compass & a little mathematics. <u>Thus</u> I got my first practice in giving orders & gradually I get

---

[1] Thomas was back at London Headquarters for a short time, from about the end of October, before heading to Hare Hall Camp on November 15.

less confidential in tone. Possibly they may want me to stick to this job indefinitely. Map-reading & the use of the compass are very important for tactics & artillery work, & all officers are supposed to be able to do a useful map or field sketch to scale on the spot in quick time. So there have to be instructors & if I can feel myself useful I can (if I wish) give up or postpone my intention of taking a commission. At any rate I shall not be a commissioned officer as soon as I thought. But I expect I shall find it easy to decide before very long to give up the instructor's job & take a commission, unless it seems pure vanity to do so. I mean that strictly speaking it is more reasonable to remain at home doing necessary work that I can do than going out & trying my hand at something that perhaps I can't do. On the other hand it isn't easy to know whether the doubt in my mind is due to a feeling that I ought to go out as an officer or simply to the knowledge that most people will think less of me as a corporal at home than a lieutenant abroad.

Now I must go down. Helen has had influenza & is out of condition. She is waiting down at the cottage. We are getting November sunshine now on still gorgeous woods. The two girls are well. The garden is full. But news is all bad. I am ready for another letter from you.

Maitland Radford is next door (rereading 'North of Boston' & liking it, Helen says) & comes in often. Sometimes Eleanor Farjeon or his mother is there. You heard perhaps that he finished the year he signed for as an army doctor & came back rather wrecked. I didn't see him then. He is still resting. He twitches far more than he used, but talks the same.

Monro tells me Hulme was wounded slightly, came home, was offered a commission in an infantry regiment which he didn't want & is still at home.

It is a pity Rupert Brooke is the only poet killed. I mean a pity for us readers.

4 & 20 Blackbirds is out with a feeble frontispiece. 'Marlborough' is out: so is 'This England' (anthology). They are getting friendly

useless reviews. But who cares? Books are published <u>now</u> because publishers know things can only get worse as time goes on.

Mervyn didn't stay on then. It would have been pleasant for us if he had come straight from you. But you know I am not grumbling or thinking anything about it. It was entirely for you to decide.

Now I am going to trim the hedge & have tea with Bronwen while Helen fetches Baba from a dancing class. Baba said the other day: 'The only thing I should like to be <u>in the way of men</u> is a Scottie with a kilt.' I asked what she would like to be 'in the way of women' & she said: 'A widow.'

12 months ago I was coming over to you from Wales in the rain with my boil. I hope I shall see you before another 12 months are out, & I shan't mind if the time has come for another boil. Goodbye. Our love to all of you. I hope you are going to get easily through the winter. I am off to camp again probably in a week, a different camp, I am not sure where.

Yours ever
Edward Thomas.

43. Thomas to Frost

Friday *Steep*

13 xi[1] *Petersfield*

My dear Robert

I am on my way home again for a day before going into camp on Monday. No one much wants to go into camp in low country in Essex only 12 miles from London, & in the winter, but they say it is a particularly good camp. The huts &c were prepared for the Sportsman's Battalion & filled up at unusual expense by some of the rich members of the Battalion.

I said, didn't I, that this would be a preparation for New Hampshire, & it turns out to be so in an unexpected way. For the time being I am a schoolmaster superintending the work of men during lectures on map-reading & map-making, & also taking out parties of men & helping them to construct maps in the field or to enlarge and add to printed maps. So I certainly shall be much less afraid of teaching in your summer school after this period of teaching things I know rather little about. When I have had a month or two of it I shall be ready for a commission & have special qualifications that I should not have had if I had taken one now like most of my contemporaries. Of course if I wished I could probably stay on indefinitely as an instructor. The question is whether I ought to stick to the soft job luck has put in my way. I shall let it decide itself, or rather it will decide itself.

---

[1] Friday would have been the 12th of November.

I have just been sending Scott the money for Mervyn's fare over here. It makes Christmas seem very near & I haven't looked forward to a Christmas so for very many years. If anything occurs to you between the times when this reaches you & Mervyn starts, you will write to Scott, won't you? Anything about choice of steamers or time of traveling, way of getting to New York, for example. It doesn't matter how soon he returns, but we want it to be well in time for Christmas. Soon after the new year I expect he will go to Hodson's school & stay 2 or 3 terms.

Marching back from Hampstead today I had an actor next me who had been out in the States early this year acting in 'Rutherford & Son' &c & he told me of a Yankee who couldn't hear him on the telephone & said 'Snow again, I couldn't catch your drift'. I asked him about New Hampshire but he only remembered a railway station that reminded him of some story of Kipling's.

Last night I stopped with an Oxford Press friend of J.C. Smith's. Smith is in London (alone) doing work in connection with munitions & we are to meet. There is a scheme for him & me to collaborate in an anthology of narrative poems, but I really can't apply myself to that kind of thing now. Ever since I have been in London with a comfortable room of an evening I haven't been able to read at all, except technical things. I am sure it is a very great relief. I never was so well or in so balanced a mood. I am quite vain with satisfaction at doing what I did 4 months ago: it is just 4 months. I don't look ahead with any anxiety. I just look forward without a thought to something, I don't know what, I don't speculate what. But I can tell you that the only element I am conscious of when I look forward is New Hampshire. I realize—I think no more about it—that England will be no place for me when all is over, though of course things may happen. Don't forget about the school, will you?

Goodbye now. Perhaps I will write some more when I get to Steep. It is a slow & shaky train.

The day's over, a cold blowing day bright all the time after a storm of wind in the night & rain in the day. Helen & I have been up to the study to light a fire. Maitland Radford & I have been up that way again with 2 naval lieutenants who turned up, one an old acquaintance of mine & Hodgson's, the other a peaceable British Museum man looking very much a lamb in his sea-wolf's clothing—they were pleased to see our hangers mostly bare now except the yellow larch & the dark yew, after being 7 months at sea. Coming back I tried to paint Hodgson for Radford. Did I tell you Hodgson was in the Anti-aircraft service? They say he has mostly been doing cook's work: the guns didn't suit him & he was over 10 years older than the next oldest man there.

I wonder would you recognise me with hair cropped close & carrying a thin little swagger cane: many don't who meet me unexpectedly, & they say I never looked so well in health. Now you will think me getting over to the other extreme of complacency. But I am not. Coming in home last night after walking home fast in the rain at 10 & finding the place upside down & Helen almost as much scared & surprised as pleased to see me, I went down plump to the old level. I had been too eager & enjoyed the rain too much—with solitary excitement. Does one really get rid of things at all by steadily inhibiting them for a long time on end? Is peace going to awaken me as it will so many from a drugged sleep? Am I indulging in the pleasure of being someone else?

I have got to be off early tomorrow to pack & get ready & see a little of my mother before leaving her alone. My father is away & the only brother living at home is also in the Artists & going to camp with me on Monday.

Goodbye to you all.

Ever yours
Edward Thomas

44. Frost to Thomas

Franconia N H.
November 23 1915

Dear Edward

I have reached a point this evening where no letter to or from you will take the place of seeing you. I am simply down on the floor kicking and thrashing with resentment against everything as it is. I like nothing, neither being here with you there and so hard to talk to nor being so ineffectual at my years to help myself or anyone else. How am I going to tell you in cold writing that I tried to place your Four-and-twenty Blackbirds with Holt and failed. I know it was something I didnt say or do to bear down the publishers doubts of the book as too English for the American mother and child. It is not too English—someone will see it yet—and I tried to make the publishers see it by not saying too much and by not saying too little. But if I havent succeeded in doing any thing for you, I haven't succeeded in doing anything for myself. If I seem to have made any headway with the American reading crowd, it is by what was done for me before I left England. You over there brought it about that I was named the other day in the "Queries" department of a school paper as perhaps the equal of Ella Wheeler Wilcox and James Whitcomb Riley. Don't think I am bitter. You know how little I ask. Only I wish I could have the credit for getting a little of it for myself and perhaps sharing a little of it with someone else. I havent even dug in on this farm yet. I am still a beggar for the roof over our heads. And you know how it is with us; Elinor is so sick day and night as to affect the judgement of both of us: we cant see anything hopefully though we know from experience that even the worst nine months must somehow come to an end. The devil says "One way or another." And thats what Elinor says too this time. There is really cause for anxiety.[1] We are not now the strength we were.[2]

Is this in the miserable confidential tone they are curing you of by manly discipline? You wont be able [to] hit it off with the like of me by the time the war is over. You'll be wondering how you ever found pleasure in grovelling with me in such self-abasement—walking about the fields of Leddington—in the days that were. Couldn't we run ourselves down then without fear of losing too much favor with each other?

Do you want me to tell you the best thing that has come to me for a long long time, let you take it as you will and act on it as you will from the will to be agreeable or from perversity. It is the news that the country may not ask of you all that you have shown yourself ready to give. I dont want you to die (I confess I wanted you to face the possibility of death): I want you to live to come over here and begin all over the life we had in St Martin's Lane at Tyler's Green at White Leaved Dale and at Balham. Use should decide it for you. If you can be more useful living than dying I dont see that you have to go behind that. Dont be run away with by your nonsense.

You know I haven't tried to be troubled by the war. But I believe it is half of what's ailed me ever since August 1914. Lately I have almost despaired of England at times. I've almost been afraid

---

[1] Referring to Elinor's pregnancy. Frost had written to Abercrombie on September 21 that "Elinor is altogether out of health and we are in for our share of trouble too. It is the old story: what she has been through so many times. . . . The doctor frightens me about her heart" (*SLRF*, p. 192). She miscarried in late November.

[2] Tennyson, "Ulysses," ll. 66–7: "We are not now that strength which in old days / Moved earth and heaven . . ."

ELECTED FRIENDS

that she might be beaten on land and brought to terms which might prove the end of her in fifty years. We say a disturbance of the balance of power was what caused the war. It shows how little the balance was really disturbed—the fight is so equal and so desperate. I agree with what Pat said to Pat and with what Pat answered. Pat said "It's a terrible war!' And Pat answered "Terrible, but after all it's better than no war at all."

I'll write you in a better vein than this within a week. Tell Baba our silly President thinks well of widows too. Damn some people that get in my light.[3]

Goodbye Soldier

R

Say something pleasant and characteristic for me to everybody not excluding Miss Farjeon and Maitland Radford.

---

[3] Possibly alluding to the anecdote about Diogenes the Cynic's asking Alexander the Great to stand out of his light. Thomas had alluded to another such anecdote in [26].

45. Thomas to Frost

6 xii 15

My dear Robert

It seems an age since I wrote & longer since I heard from you. Now it is a wet evening & everyone is playing cards & it is easy to begin a letter. We have begun real work again, each of us taking 10 or 12 men out for 5 days on end & trying to teach them the elements of map-reading, fieldsketching, the use of compass & protractor, & making a map on the ground with & without the compass. We get a fresh set every week of 5 working days. The pay is still 1/- a day, but one learns a lot, & if I decide to take a commission the experience will have been valuable. Whether I do decide depends on how I like this work & how useful I find myself. As I probably told you, everyone advises me to stick at it, at least for some months.

We don't take a class on Saturday so I have got off two Friday nights in succession, returning Sunday night. So I had a whole Saturday at Steep the week before last & did some gardening, chopped some wood & lit a fire in my study. Last Friday night I got to Coventry to talk to Hodson about Mervyn. Mervyn is to live there & attend the school for 2 terms. After that Hodson may get a commission in the Artillery. He took a course in the Cambridge Officers Training Corps last Summer vacation.

We are now hoping to hear that Mervyn's fare has reached him at East Alstead. If it has he says he will sail in the St Louis on December 10 & I can't tell you how we look forward to seeing him. Of course we don't know yet here what Xmas leave we shall have. But I hope for 3 days. I have never had more than 2 days at home on end since I joined 5 months ago, & that only twice.

Yesterday afternoon I saw de la Mare. Did I tell you Garnett had promised to see if he could get me something from the Civil List. (Davies by the way is getting his £50 doubled, they say). Well, Garnett went off to the Italian front with an ambulance party, & I imagine he forgot me. So I put my tongue in my cheek & asked de la Mare if he could put things in motion. Perhaps he will. I am first making sure that Garnett hasn't done anything.

Have you seen the 2nd Georgian Anthology? I had a faint chance of getting in. At least Bottomley wanted to show some of my things to Marsh. But they have kept in Monro. The only things I really much like are de la Mare's & perhaps Davies'. Bottomley may be all right. The new man Ledwidge isn't any good, is he? Abercrombie of course is a poet. I don't know. I couldn't really spend any time in the volume after looking to see if there was anything new in it, & except Ledwidge there wasn't. But I suppose what I think doesn't matter at all considering I read less than any man in the hut. I don't want to read anything. On the other hand as soon as I get really free with nothing close before me to do I incline to write. I have written two things here or rather 3,[1] but one was just rhyming on. —I am always just a little more outside things than most of the others without being made to feel so at all acutely. They aren't surprised whether I come in or stay out of a group.

It won't be long before Christmas when this reaches you. I hope you are all going to be together & well & glad to be there on Christ-

---

[1] Probably "There's nothing like the sun" (November 18–19), "The Thrush" (November), and "Liberty" (written on the way home from Hare Hall Camp, November 26).

mas day. We shall be thinking about you. It must somehow fall out that we don't have to live on letters very long. Give my love to Elinor & all the children.

Yours ever
Edward Thomas

III. 1916

46. Thomas to Frost

2.i.16.

My dear Robert,

I couldn't easily write during Christmas week, though I had your news then about Elinor[1] & a letter from Lesley too. For nearly a week I was at Steep with Mervyn & all. He got back on the Sunday[2] but too late for me to see him as I had to be back here by 9.15. We found him very little changed except in temper. Perhaps I had changed that way too. So we all got on well & had a very pleasant time & 3 days walking. Then on the Wednesday after Christmas I returned here to begin work on Thursday. Our old hut—I want to remember to send you a photograph of it—was broken up, the men separated. We were homeless for a time & rather miserable in the rain. Now we are settling down in a new hut, 5 of us instructors & a small crowd of recruits. The result is that, as senior man, I am in charge of the hut, & have a number of little duties thrust on me— to appoint men to fetch the food &c & to clean up the hut &c. We rather dread losing the freedom of the last 2 months.

Yesterday I got up to London (it being Saturday) for the day & saw Monro & Davies. It will be a good thing if I don't see Monro again. He seems to delight in expressing opinions that he knows won't please me, just for the sake perhaps of asserting himself. His

---

[1] Probably the news of her miscarriage.

[2] January 19.

lady is still there, very pale & said now to be consumptive. She talked about Hodgson & said he sent his love to me, so I am forgiven.[3] Davies was back from a week in Wales, & pleased with his £100 a year. He has 2 very good rooms in a decent quiet street near the Museum. Some painter has given him a picture of a stout nude seen from behind, & it hangs on his wall. He didn't think much of the new Georgian Anthology, chiefly (I believe) because the reviewers have not praised it. Privately he didn't see anything in the selections from de la Mare's 'Peacock Pie'. We agreed about Drinkwater. Even Monro & I agreed about Drinkwater.

In turn I saw my father too,—he made me very sick. He treats me so that I have a feeling of shame that I am alive. I couldn't sleep after it. Nothing much happened. We argued about the war & he showed that his real feeling when he is not trying to be nice & comfortable is one of contempt. I know what contempt is & partly what I suffered was from the reminder that I had probably made Helen feel exactly the same. I came more drearily back to camp than ever before. I shall recover, but it makes a difference & I am inclined not to see him again for a time.

But you have had a worse time. I hope it is passed & Elinor stronger & about. I shall look for your next letter to say so.

People are talking all the time. It is a wet Sunday. One man is hanging up pictures he is to show at an exhibition of pictures by the Artists Rifles. Another is discussing with me a book on our subject for immediate publication. I am lending him a hand. We must get a walk before dark & we have only been to church & back today.

Goodbye. My love to you all. By the way, I delivered scraps of a lecture impromptu the other day. There were 30 men & I didn't mind. It all helps us.

Yours ever
Edward Thomas.

---

[3] See [53] note 1.

47. Thomas to Frost

Still at Hare Hall Camp

16 i 16

My dear Robert,

Again it is an immeasurable time since I heard from you & a little less since I wrote. There is little fresh to tell you. I think I told you we were transferred to a new Company which makes us appear on parade first thing in the morning with packs & rifles, & so we move for an hour & then take up our ordinary work. Also I am responsible for the 20 men in the hut, to call the roll, see that the meals are fetched & served & cleaned up, the hut kept clean, to organise & keep a fund for buying luxuries. I got into trouble last week end through reporting a man present because I thought he would be in soon after I had to make the report. He arrived at 7 next morning & we both had two serious talks with officers. Probably my promotion will be delayed. I am now L/Cpl P.E. Thomas by the way. If the war lasts long enough I may be Sergeant. The work isn't dull yet. We go over the same ground every week—the course lasts a week—but each time we learn & vary the course. We take a separate new lot of men each week & they are always different. New work is always turning up & putting us in new positions for a time. The worst of it is I get less leave & it is harder to get. I couldn't see Mervyn yesterday on his birthday or take him to Coventry to begin school there. He went, I believe, & is to live with Hodson. Bronwen is back at home & going back to school on Monday. I may be home at the end of this week. The garden has been too sodden lately to work in. The winter has been mild & wet since the November snow. Today was a typical day. John Freeman came down to see me & we watched out through the misty cold still weather, with thrushes singing everywhere & no soul about while we ate our lunch. Yesterday all I could do was to draw two panoramas of the neighboring country. We can't go beyond the 2-mile radius unless we are on leave, nor enter a public house within the 2-mile radius, which is presumably to benefit the camp canteen. Half the men are away this week end, & the rest are out with friends, & I have had a lot of time to myself—which always tempts me to write & sometimes I do.

It is amusing. Coming home in the twilight at the end of our day's work, we four instructors march in the rear of the platoon (30 to 60 men) and sing together 'Mr John Blunt' & one or two other songs of mine. They all like 'As I was a walking down Paradise Street'[1] but you can't march to it. Of course most of the men are far junior to me in this corps. I am six months old, they are six weeks or little more. Most of our generation are officers now with various regiments, or else settled as non-commissioned officers like myself in this corps. We talk about High Beech, our former camp, & they look at [us] as part of ancient history. Beautiful those Autumn Days almost without rain seem now. This camp is perfectly arranged & equipped & we sleep in canvas beds, but we think we would rather be on the floor at High Beech. It is always raining here & the clay holds all the wet & the camp is on perfect flat. Still the country round is low wooded hills & no villas. That is the advantage of clay: you don't get villas on it, & except on spots valuable for big factories you have simply farms, forges, inns, cottages & big houses very often old. We find pleasant walks when we do have a day off, which is the next best thing to having leave to go where we like by road or rail.

Such an endless variety of men & accents & names. There is one with a voice like Gibson. I want to know where he comes from.

---

[1] Better known as "Blow the Man Down."

Business men, clerks, teachers, pianists, schoolboys, colonials, men who fought under Botha last year, all mixed up & made indistinguishable at first by the uniform. Until you know a new man fairly well you think of him simply as a soldier. I daresay I have been mistaken for one myself—[.] Well, I can keep step & set a step too, & though I dislike inflicting discipline I can submit to it pretty well & don't ask questions so often as many do or complain of the unreasonableness of rules, of the war, of life & so on. Goodbye.

Yours ever
Edward Thomas

48. Thomas to Frost

Sunday 30 i 16

My dear Robert,

I wish you would write. I am not greatly enjoying things just now. Baba has been ill. The weather has been muggy. Also I have just been denied the promotion to corporal which I should have had, & which the man I work with has had. This puts him over me & though he is as nice as could be about it I don't enjoy it. It seems the offence I told you about a fortnight ago was taken very seriously & this is my punishment. It helps to make me conscious of not succeeding very well in my work here. I certainly don't. I often fail utterly to teach the men anything. Well, I won't go on like this, but I felt inclined to volunteer for France when 300 were asked for last week, & I still hope we may (all of us instructors) go if only for a time just to get me out of this camp to a different kind of mind.

I got home a week ago for 24 hours. Now this week end has to be spent in camp with no work to do except look after the hut while my superior is away. These are the worst days. The only real cure is to get quite alone & write. I can sometimes get the hut empty & write. Then I sometimes write in the train going home late. I must send you one or 2 recent verses. 'Lob' & 'Words' are to appear in a big hotchpotch called 'Form' in March.[1] Otherwise I keep out of print.

---

[1] *Form, A Quarterly of the Arts* (April 1916), edited by Austin O. Spare and Francis Marsden. The poems appeared under the name Edward Eastaway.

The men are still very amusing, especially the worst man in the hut, a big frank half-mad degenerate who does what he pleases. Now he is fondling me to get something out of me. I must shut up & hope to get a letter sent from Steep before long, telling me some news. Goodbye

Yours ever
Edward Thomas.

49. Thomas to Frost
21 ii 16   *Hare Hall Camp*

My dear Robert,

What have I done that you shouldn't write to me for a month or more? You treat me worse than the sergeant-major does or did when he refused to have me made a full corporal. For what does a stripe more or less, sewn on your sleeve, matter?

At any rate I hear we are to meet in spirit. Bottomley said I was to contribute to a poetic annual planned by Trevelyan, Abercrombie & others; & he said he believed you would too.[1] But it isn't enough that Robert Frost should be printed somewhere near Edward Eastaway of the other Hampshire. So please write & say either that I am forgiven or that 3 or 4 letters have been lost in the post.

Mervyn had a letter from Lesley not long ago which said you & Elinor were in Boston. I hope Elinor is resting & you are doing a lot of business there. I wish it was Monro was in Boston & you in Devonshire Street,[2] tho you might not like the bombs they get thereabouts. Do you know he told Mr Ellis that he felt he was doing a useful or necessary thing (words to that effect) in continuing the Poetry Bookshop. He really did. I mean I believe he did. It is what Belloc calls extremely rum. Davies was going to tea with him the other day when I called. He said Monro had asked him & as he

---

[1] *An Annual of New Poetry 1917* printed eighteen poems by Thomas under his pseudonym Edward Eastaway, as well as six poems by Frost.

[2] The address of Monro's Poetry Bookshop.

hadn't been there for a long time he thought he would go in case Monro should think there was something up.

I have had a bit of a holiday lately. I took a chill somehow & had to take to bed in my father's house. Then I had 4 days convalescence at home which was better than nothing. I am not up to the mark yet & I finish up the day tired.

Saturday night & a few hours on either side of it I spent with Mervyn at Hodson's house. Mervyn likes it better than he used to like school & talks about his work rather more. He seems to be feeling ahead & getting ready to do something.

Now the hut has filled up & some are playing cards & some talking about the rate of pay being in inverse ratio to the amount of risk run, & so on. I can't write any more yet. Now they have got onto the measles. There is an epidemic in camp, & we all dread it getting to our hut, which would mean we should be isolated & confined to this camp & unable to go home till 18 days after the last case.

I had an offer the other day to write the history of a regiment. Of course I cannot take it till the war is over, & then I expect it might be wise not to hang on here picking up odd jobs. If I can & if nothing unexpected turns up, I shall come straight out to you. Goodbye. My love to you & Elinor & the children.

Yours ever
E.T.

50. Thomas to Frost

March 5   *Hare Hall Camp*

My dear Robert

No one can have Patience who pursues Glory, so you will have to toss up with Eleanor which vice you shall claim in public.

Well, I was hoping your silence meant you had something better to do than write letters. When they told me you would contribute to the Annual I thought it likely. Now I am glad to hear it is so, but sorry to have to wait for the Annual before seeing the poems. I don't know if you got them, but I have sent several from time to time. Your not mentioning them made me think I had missed fire. I have written so many I suppose I am always missing fire.

I have done nothing like your lecture at Lawrence.[1] As soon as I stand up & look at 30 men I can do nothing but crawl backwards & forwards between the few points I can still remember under the strain. It will mean a long war if I am to improve. You ask if I think it is going to be a long war. I don't think, but I do expect a lot of unexpected things & am not beginning really to look forward to any change. I hardly go beyond assuming that the war will end.

We have been through a time of change here lately. In fact we may not be out of it yet. I was not sure if the reconstruction would have me out & compel me to take a commission. Today it seems more likely we shall go on as we were. Even so, if I have to wait much longer for promotion I shall be inclined to throw this job

---

[1] Frost gave a talk on "The Sound of Poetry" in Lawrence, MA on January 19, 1916.

up. I have been restless lately. Partly the annoyance of my promotion being delayed. Partly the rain & the long hours indoors. Partly my 10 days chill. Then there has been measles in the camp for 6 weeks & now we have it & are isolated & denied our leave this week which includes my birthday when I meant to be at Steep.

This should only improve what you condemn as my fastidious taste in souls. Yet soul is a word I feel I can't have used for years & years. Anyhow here I have to like people because they are more my sort than the others, although I realise at certain times they are not my sort at all & will vanish away after the war. What almost completes the illusion is that I can't help talking to them as if they were friends.

Partly what made me restless was the desire to write, without the power. It lasted 5 or 6 weeks till yesterday I rhymed some.[2]

Your talking of epic & play rather stirred me. I shall be careful not to <u>indulge</u> in a spring run of lyrics. I had better try again to make other people speak. I suppose I take it easily, especially now when it is partly an indulgence. —I wish you would send some of yours without bargaining.

Well, the long & short of it seems to be that I am what I was, in spite of my hopes of last July. The only thing is perhaps I didn't quite know what I was. This less active life you see gives me more time & inclination to ruminate. Also it is Sunday, always a dreary ruminating day if spent in camp. We got a walk, three of us, one a schoolmaster, the other a game-breeder who knows about horses & dogs & ferrets. We heard the first blackbird, walked 9 or 10 miles straight across country (the advantage of our uniform—we go just where we like): ate & drank (stout) by a fire at a big quiet inn— not a man to drink left in the village: drew a panorama—a landscape for military purposes drawn exactly with the help of a compass & a protractor, which is an amusement I have quite taken to—they say I am a neo-realist at it.

---

[2] "Celandine."

Abercrombie wrote a nice letter about some of my verses he had seen. Nobody's compliments would <u>flatter</u> me so much or more.

I can't go on with this now because everything is upside down. We don't know who or where or what we are. We five don't want to be split up & scattered. On the other hand we may each be made independent & put in charge of a company & so get rapid promotion.

Goodbye. They are all well at home, & Mervyn at Coventry. I was to have gone home for my birthday last week. Eleanor Farjeon was there. Now I have a chance of going this week end. My presents are waiting for me. But one of the best things I had on the day was your letter—a lucky accident. Give my love to them all & I hope I shall see them before I am still another year older.

Yours ever
Edward Thomas

51. Thomas to Frost

Hare Hall Camp

March 16 16

My dear Robert

Your letter of February 24 only reached me yesterday. It referred to some verses I had sent—dismal ones, I gather. Perhaps one was called 'Rain', a form of excrement you hoped it was when you said 'work all that off in poetry & I shan't complain'. Well, I never know. I was glad to know of a letter reaching you. I had begun to fear perhaps my letters didn't reach you. Lately I was able to write again. But I got home on Saturday & left them there. If I can find the rough draft here I will copy one out.[1]

Things are still difficult here. There has been a complete re-organisation. We do not know how it will affect us ultimately. So far it has meant that we only instruct the company (D) to which we have been attached since Xmas, whereas we used to instruct the whole battalion of 4 companies in turn. Our sergeant has gone, left us, so the corporal who would have been my junior is now in charge of us & may get made a sergeant & leave me still as I was. We are very busy. I lecture twice a day. Nearly all the work is indoors, & the weather is changing at last. The snow has melted. The sun is very warm. The rooks in the camp trees are nesting. They wake us at 5.30. We turn out for physical drill at 6.30. I have made myself fire-lighter now. We are 4 non-commissioned officers in one hut

---

[1] "Home" ("Fair was the morning . . . "), and "Thaw."

& N.C.O.'s are not supposed to do anything menial, which is hard on the other men, there being usually only one N.C.O in a hut of 25 or 30. So to appease them I light the 2 stoves while they are still in bed, & so far the Lord has been on my side, my fires are wonderful. That is where my modesty fails, you perceive.

Yes I knew it was a year ago you went away, & two since Tyler's Green;—& one before what? But Ledington, my dear Robert, in April, in June, in August.

It is warm today. We have a day with no work (but plenty to consider) & 2 of us are left in the parlour of 'The Shepherd & Dog' 2 miles from camp, a public house rather like that one at Tyler's Green or Penn. I am writing this & the other man, who is an artist, is trying to draw me.[2] The taproom is very noisy, but here there is only a fire & 3 billiard balls on a table & us. He is the man through whom I fell into disgrace. I haven't outlived it yet. But now there is a chance my senior may go to another company & leave me in charge of D. The worst of it is he & I are very good pals and if we are in different companies we can't see nearly so much of one another. This means a lot because most of the men around are going to be officers soon & fresh ones will arrive & take their places & then still another set arrive.

You might have sent me Flint's address. I hardly know where to find it, unless through Monro.

I heard from de la Mare lately. He has been talking to Newbolt about a pension for me. Newbolt he says isn't very hopeful.

When I was at home I picked out 40 poems & sent them to Bottomley to pick out as many as he likes to fill 15 or 20 pages.[3]

The news nowadays is pretty good. It looks as if we could stand any battering the Germans inflict & as if we might yet give them a battering they could not stand. There is a prophecy abroad that it

---

[2] John Wheatley's sketch is reproduced in *GB*, facing page 178.

[3] Bottomley was to help choose which of Thomas's poems would be included in *An Annual of New Poetry*.

will be over by July 17. Helen says Why not by her birthday, which is a few days earlier? She would be more pleased than I. She has had enough of the war & of comparative solitude[.]

Well, we had to leave the inn (being soldiers) at 2.30. We drew a panorama (you must see some some day) & got back to the usual thing & the news that my brother has got his 2nd stripe on his sleeve, i.e. is a full corporal. These reminders that I am going to be passed over all the time don't please me, especially at the end of a soft moist warm day, the first such day since last April. But I am yours ever

Edward Thomas

52. Frost, "Not to Keep"[1]

Not to Keep

They sent him back to her. The letter came
Saying . . . And she could have him. And before
She could be sure there was no hidden ill
Under the formal writing, he was there,
Living. They gave him back to her alive—
How else? They are not known to send the dead—
And not disfigured visibly. His face?
His hands? She had to look, to look and ask,
'What is it, dear?' And she had given all
And still she had all—*they* had—they the lucky!
Wasn't she glad now? Everything seemed won,
And all the rest for them permissible ease.
She had to ask, 'What was it, dear?'

                                        'Enough
Yet not enough. A bullet through and through,
High in the breast. Nothing but what good care
And medicine and rest, and you a week,
Can cure me of to go again.' The same

---

[1] Sent along with a letter, which I have failed to locate, dated May 1, 1916 (see [53]). The poem, first published in *The Yale Review* for January 1917 and later included in *New Hampshire*, is not about Thomas, but was evidently inspired by him.

Grim giving to do over for them both.
She dared no more than ask him with her eyes
How was it with him for a second trial.
And with his eyes he asked her not to ask.
They had given him back to her, but not to keep.

53. Thomas to Frost
May 21

My dear Robert,

This last letter of your[s] (dated May 1) with the poem 'Not to Keep' mends all, though it was opened (& untouched) by the censor. I hadn't been able to write to you for some weeks simply because I didn't know where to join on. I began to fear the censor had been a Hodgson patriot[1] & found something rotten in me or my verses. However, all's well—we don't care a b—[2] do we? To use 2 phrases which an Irishman in our hut used to make seem so witty. He had a face like an archaic Greek god's that people had trodden on for 1000 years. Now he has gone to France to see if he can still be witty.

'Not to keep' is all right. It is no disadvantage to you to be 40. Of course one would prefer to be able to run a mile in 5 minutes & jump a spiked fence, but actually I find less to grumble at out loud than 10 years ago: I suppose I am more bent on making the best of what I have got instead of airing the fact that I deserve so much more. Yet I feel old—I felt old seeing Bottomley's 'Lear', Gibson's 'Hoops', & Rupert Brooke's 'Lithuania', yesterday afternoon. Bottomley's play, for example. It was all the result of thinking out an explanation for what might very likely be a fact. He had to make

---

[1] Thomas wrote to Gordon Bottomley, January 30, 1915, that he and Hodgson were "not meeting till the war is over. I am not patriotic enough for his exuberant taste" (*GB*, p. 243).

[2] A joke at the censor's expense?

Goneril run a knife through a rabbit's eyes. Well, I firmly believe that if he had imagination he would have kept such a thing dark supposing he could go the length of imagining it. As it was, it sounded just a thought out cruelty, worse far than cruelty itself with passion behind it. Of course he pretended there was passion. There wasn't. Brooke was better though he was only painting with Russian paints. I quite admired the simple souls who couldn't help laughing. —I mean I felt old because I believed I saw how it was done though I don't suppose I could do it myself as well or better if at all.

Nobody recognises me now. Sturge Moore, E. Marsh, & R. C. Trevelyan stood a yard off & I didn't trouble to awake them to stupid recognition. Bottomley & his wife I just had a word with. I was with a young artist named Paul Nash who has just joined us as a map reader. He is a change from the 2 schoolmasters I see most of. He is wonderful at finding birds' nests. There is another artist, too, aged 24, a Welshman, absolutely a perfect Welshman, kind, simple, yet all extremes & rather unreal & incredible except in his admirations—he admires his wife & Rembrandt for example. I am really lucky to have such a crowd of people always round & these 2 or 3 nearer: you might guess from "Home"[3] how much nearer.

Though I am Corporal P.E. Thomas I am not growing so efficient as all that. We don't get a chance. We idle away for days together for lack of organisation. Shall I copy out the speech our captain made to the men who were leaving us to go to be finished at the cadet school? 'Pay attention. Stand easy. I just want to say a few words to you men who are going to the school. I wish you all success. I hope you won't get into any trouble at all. Take care to mind your Ps & Qs, & do everything top-hole.' He is a kind huge man with no memory, very fond of the country. The other day in

---

[3] Thomas's third poem of this title ("Fair was the morning . . . "), composed in early March 1916. See especially lines 22–24: ". . . and we knew we were not friends / But fellows in a union that ends / With the necessity for it, as it ought."

the fields he said 'Company, attention! Oh, look at that rabbit.' I wish we could win a little sooner. Then I could come & see you barn-storming. Also I could perhaps begin to earn money. They are going to relieve some soldiers to the extent of £2 a week, but only those who joined <u>after</u> last August 15. So I don't count. They had to put some limit. Perhaps they thought the waiters had more to give up. Or they want to encourage the last. Don't you worry though, about money. Something may happen. A pension or grant is still just possible, tho de la Mare says improbable:—I am not old enough is his explanation. Also I may possibly get a job which will take me out into the fighting line yet not into the worst risks & give me more money—as an officer. Of course anything may happen now. Things are continually being shaken up & one drops through a hole or not. You make sure of your farm. If I did want money I would ask you, but I have £100 of war loan left.

Yes, I wear 2 stripes or chevrons on my upper arm now—not on the skin, but the sleeve.

Haines writes occasionally with news of the great & lately a persuasion to review Doughty's last, which I did.[4] I can't get to see him. He is too far for any short leaves. I go home everytime. Mervyn was the last time. He hasn't got on with Hodson & we are all uncertain what to do. I am thinking of asking acquaintances in Wales if he could go into Steel Works there. He isn't much changed & still shows only his apathy. The others are well. As I was walking home with Helen & Baba last week, Baba asked whether M^{rs} —'s baby was a boy or a girl. 'A boy.' 'Everyone has boys'. But I said boys were wanted to replace the dead. 'You don't think I haven't heard that before, my lad, do you?' she said to me. She is acquisitive & not generous, but she gets her own way without arguing much. I have some new songs for her from camp, & rather more for you.

---

[4] Charles M. Doughty, *The Titans* (1916).

Goodbye & my love to all of you. Elinor is well, isn't she? Don't forget to send any photographs you have of all or any of you & the farm ground.

Yours ever
Edward Thomas

You should have seen Monro in the vestibule of the theatre selling Bottomley's 'Lear',[5] standing up straight & just pursuing the women with the whites of his eyes[.]

---

[5] Bottomley's play had been printed in Monro's anthology, *Georgian Poetry 1913–15.*

54. Thomas, "The sun used to shine"[1]

The sun used to shine

The sun used to shine while we two walked
Slowly together, paused and started
Again, and sometimes mused, sometimes talked
As either pleased, and cheerfully parted

Each night. We never disagreed
Which gate to rest on. The to be
And the late past we gave small heed.
We turned from men or poetry

To rumours of the war remote
Only till both stood disinclined
For aught but the yellow flavorous coat
Of an apple wasps had undermined;

Or a sentry of dark betonies,
The stateliest of small flowers on earth,
At the forest verge; or crocuses
Pale purple as if they had their birth

---

[1] Composed at Hare Hall Camp on May 22, 1916.

In sunless Hades fields. The war
Came back to mind with the moonrise
Which soldiers in the east afar
Beheld then. Nevertheless, our eyes

Could as well imagine the Crusades
Or Caesar's battles. Everything
To faintness like those rumours fades—
Like the brook's water glittering

Under the moonlight—like those walks
Now—like us two that took them, and
The fallen apples, all the talks
And silences—like memory's sand

When the tide covers it late or soon,
And other men through other flowers
In those fields under the same moon
Go talking and have easy hours.

55. Thomas to Frost

10 vi 16   *Hare Hall Camp*

My dear Robert,

I like all these poems, but particularly 'An Old Man's Winter Night', 'Out, out', and 'An Encounter'.[1] Is the 'Encounter' from the South? I like to remember you talk of the South as much as anything local. 'Not to Keep' is more like an abridgement of part of a play. That is what occurs to me after liking it. Are you actually attempting plays now as well as sowing peas? Our peas are fairly well up but most things have done shockingly. It nearly broke my heart to see the garden last weekend. But now the Government instead of a pension is going to give me £300 in a lump. This will simplify some things. Mervyn's case, for example, especially as my engineer brother[2] has promised to get him into a big motor works on Sept. 1 & this is being settled.

Also I am rather expecting I may get a commission before very long as an officer in the Anti-Aircraft Corps. It will mean a term of training in gunnery in London. My map-reading will help.

We are now working pretty steadily here. But you wouldn't believe how much more importance they keep attaching to smartness—in drill, dress, & brightness of all brass things in dress & equipment. It may be right. One notices only the time spent on it.

---

[1] All three poems were collected in *Mountain Interval*, which was published in November 1916.

[2] His brother Theodore arranged for Mervyn to train at the London Transport engineering works in Walthamstow.

Did I tell you I saw Bottomley's 'Lear' acted? The acting was shocking, but I suspect that in any case the play is not good. It is made up. B. had thought out the motives. A good deal, too, of what he must have thought best was ineffectual when spoken.

We are in for a wet turn after the heat. Warm & wet. But we walk when we can & now & again I must settle down & work something out. I must send you one or two things more.

That Annual of Trevelyan's & Abercrombie's is perhaps being hung up. So unless 'Form' does appear I shall remain unpublished.[3] I am accumulating such a mass of verses & I have an affection for so many.

Eleanor Farjeon has whooping cough but in a mild form which merely keeps her away from friends who have never had it. Margaret Radford was at Steep last week. I wish I knew whether the world was really as she sees it or why she sees it so. Maitland is working at a hospital near London now.

One of the instructors here in mapreading now is an artist named Paul Nash who remembers you.[4]

That £300 would help me to come out to you if the war were over as soon as people are now talking of. But the only certain thing is that the unexpected will happen.

Goodbye & my love to you all

Ever yours
Edward Thomas

---

[3] *Form* was meant for publication in April, but through some hitch was delayed until about mid-July.

[4] Frost and Nash had met briefly in 1913.

56. Thomas to Frost

My dear Robert,

A new step I have taken makes a good moment for writing. I offered myself for Artillery & today I was accepted, which means I shall go very soon to an Artillery school & be out in France or who knows where in a few months. After months of panic & uncertainty I feel much happier again except that I don't take easily to the trigonometry needed for artillery calculations. I have done very nearly all that I could do here in the way of teaching, lecturing, & taking charge of men in & out of doors. My old acquaintances were mostly moving out. The speeding up of things left no chance of enjoying the walks we used to have. So I had to go. Now with luck I may find myself at a School in London before firing my course, & in London I can see a few people.

There are to be other changes. Mervyn goes to Walthamstow (near Epping Forest & our old camp, & 10 miles or so N.E. of London) in early September—as an apprentice in the big Electric train, tube & bus works there; & Helen wants him to live at home. So we shall probably move. When we know where we shall be I will tell you. Meantime <u>Steep will always be a safe address</u>.

Things are going right now. We have endured long waiting. I think we can stand anything now, even success.

Of course I can't write any more verses just now & have not done for a month or so. The last I did were during a 3 days' walk that Helen & I took at the end of June when I had a few days leave due to me. We had fine bright weather & saw Ellis & a few others in Sussex & Kent. It was too short. I can only be content now in regular almost continual work when I have no time for comparisons.

Scott-James is here now, a recruit of 4 weeks old. He too is going to the Artillery. I have also come across an old Oxford acquaintance newly home from 10 years in California. He lost a child in the Lusitania & put off coming over. I suppose Monro may turn up if he is left any choice as to where he shall go.

No news. My mother has lately been operated on for cataract & is in a nursing home waiting to see again. She is not happy over my new chance of going out as an officer—I ought to be an officer in less than a few months. Nor is Helen. She is not often happy now. She is tired & anxious.

How is Carol now? I was so very sorry to hear he was making you anxious.[1] Will you write again about everything & anything? I shall so soon perhaps be out of reach of many letters. Goodbye.

Give my love to Elinor & all of them.

Yours ever
Edward Thomas.

---

[1] Carol had been consistently ill in Franconia, and his doctor thought it could possibly be tuberculosis.

57. Frost to Thomas

Franconia N.H.
August 15 1916

Dear Edward:

First I want to give you an accounting. I got here a year ago last March, didn't I? I have earned by poetry alone in the year and a half about a thousand dollars—it never can happen again—and by lecturing nearly another thousand. It has cost us more than it used to to live—partly on account of the war and partly on account of the ill health of the youngsters. Still one feels that we ought to have something to show for all that swag; and we have: we have this farm bought and nearly paid for. Such is poetry when the right people boom it. I dont say how much longer the boom can last. You can fool some of the people some of the time, but you can't fool all of them all the time, as Lincoln more or less put it. It may be that the gulfs will wash us down. Nevertheless what we have done, we have done[1] (and may He within Himself make it pure, as the poem has it[2]).

I was going to add that nobody can take it away from us. But that's not so absolutely certain. Mrs Nutt threatens from the right flank.[3]

---

[1] Tennyson, "Ulysses," ll. 62, 66–7: "It may be that the gulfs will wash us down . . . ", "We are not now that strength which in old days / Moved earth and heaven; that which we are, we are . . ."

[2] Tennyson, "Morte D'Arthur," ll. 244–5: "I have lived my life, and that which I have done / May He within Himself make pure!"

[3] See [19] note 3.

The what-shall-I-call-her has never given me one cent or one word of accounting since she took my first book. The lawyers say she has forfeited all claim on me. She can get nothing out of me. But she can make me trouble and expense if she wants to go to expense herself. I tell you that so that you will know the whole story. I may have to put the farm into my wife's name for protection. Some day soon I'll have Lesley make you a copy of the lawyer's advice in the matter.

Whats mine is yours. I say that from the heart, dear man. I may be a bad letter writer. I have been spoiled for letter writing by a mob of new friends who don't care what becomes of me so long as they get my autograph once in so often. My whole nature simply leaps at times to cross the ocean to see you for one good talk. It seems as if I couldn't bear it not to follow my inclination. I had a thought of you trying to induct me into clay pipes[4] and all the old days swept back over me. I can never live here any more without longing for there, nor there without longing for here. What kind of predicament do you call that?

But as I said, what's mine is yours. Here are a house and forty odd acres of land you can think of as a home and a refuge when your war is over. We shall be waiting for you.

My interest in the war news has picked up of late. Lloyd George is a great man. I have wanted to do some thing for your cause if it came in my way to. I thought of writing to the papers, but everybody was taking all the space and drowning everybody else out. I did my first material bit the other day when I read to a small audience for "the wounded in France"—not for the Red Cross. A collection of a hundred dollars was taken up. I'm to read twice more within a week for the same cause. I only mention this in self defense. I believe the money reaches its destination through Edith Wharton our novelist who is living in France.

Dorothy Canfield Fisher one of our good writers whom you should know has gone to France with her husband and two babies

---

[4] Thomas was fond of smoking pipes.

to help what she can. Her husband has organized a repair shop for automobile ambulances. She will be into something herself before long. Not all of us are indifferent. You should hear the standard Bostonian on the subject of the Fryatt case.[5]

Send me more poetry when you have any. I have a long thing about Snow you might care for a little.[6] I wonder if it would be likely to get to you.

It seems to me Merfyn is going the best way. I'm just Yankee enough to be sure of that.

I saw yesterday the two friends, Mrs and Miss Tilley, who had him with them in New York before he sailed. They said the loveliest things of him. They are Southerners of the old school and see nothing in anyone who is not first of all "gentle". They were evidently pleased with Merfyn for the pleasure he made them believe they gave him.

Do you think you could help me get up an anthology of the homely in poetry to be called The Old Cloak after the poem of that name?[7] Or are you too busy? I should want to claim a place on the title page along with you for my part in having got up the idea (great idea). But you would have to think of most of the material.

About time I heard from you again.

My love to you as you look in that last tall picture Helen sent.

Always and forever yours
Robert Frost.

---

[5] Fryatt was the captain of an English merchantman who attacked a German submarine in accordance with what many believed to be unlawful orders from Winston Churchill.

[6] "Snow," first published in the November issue of *Poetry*, and then in *Mountain Interval*.

[7] A sixteenth-century poem by an anonymous author.

58. Thomas to Frost

13 Rusham Rd.
Balham
London SW.

15 viii 16

My dear Robert

This will be our best address in future. We are leaving Steep to give Mervyn a home near his work, & we have not yet decided on the new cottage. It may be at High Beech, a few yards from my first camp. I have had you all in mind continually these last few days. For I have been at Steep on sick leave after vaccination, which gave me headaches &c for a week. Much of the time I spent in sorting letters, papers & books, as I may not have a home for some time to come. Helen & the children are going to the seaside. I may go at any moment to my new unit which may be in London & may be anywhere. They will move during September & soon after that I might be far off. This waiting troubles me. I really want to be out. However, I daresay I shan't be till the winter. I wrote some lines after a period in hospital[1]—largely because to concentrate is the only happy thing possible when one is bored & helpless. Today came a chance of getting a book out. A brother in law of De la Mare's[2] publishes in a small way & I am to send him a batch to look at. De la Mare talks of going out to America in October. I hope you will see him at last.

---

[1] "The Swifts."

[2] Roger Ingpen.

No news of Haines since he joined.

Eleanor Farjeon is roaming round in the fine weather. Somebody said today that one realised the blessings of peace & leisure now. I contradicted him. I don't believe I often had as good times as I have had, one way & another, these past 13 months. My faggot pile is pretty nearly used up, but it wasn't fair. We have been saving coal by wood fires out of doors, or it would have lasted the war out I believe.[3]

I want to see your handwriting again soon, though I have seen so much of it these past few days with the address Ledington, Ryton, Beaconsfield.

I brought a big load of books up with me to sell today & am sending away 2 more cases. I burnt a pile that would have roasted a sheep 2 nights ago.

No news of anyone. Hudson is still an invalid, I fear. Garnett is away. I have not seen him for 14 months. Bottomley I may see at the end of the month when everyone is away & I may have some leave between leaving my old corps & joining the new. I should like to go up there & bathe in the lake with the bird's eye primroses & the silver sand. There is nothing like the solitude of a solitary lake in early morning, when one is in deep still water. More adjectives here than I allow myself now & fewer verbs.

Goodbye all & my love to you all.

Ever yours
Edward Thomas.

---

[3] See his poem, "Fifty Faggots," in his letter to Frost of May 15, 1915 [23].

59. Thomas to Frost

13 Rusham Rd[1]
Balham
London SW.

9 ix 16

My dear Robert,

Three days ago came your letter dated August 15. So I have still a hope that mine (with some M.S.) sent about the end of July reached you just after you wrote. I have not been a good letter writer. But you know the reason. I have had no peace of mind since May. I have been busier & I have had more to think about. Now I have been 2 weeks in the Artillery learning about guns and wearing spurs &c. I think when I wrote I was down with vaccination. And I still am. I suppose it is the vaccination. I was run down. I was not careful. I got a poisoned hand.[2] I am still poor & feeble & it is very nearly all I can do to keep on with the work here, tho it is not hard physically. I learned to aim at invisible targets, to know the parts of a gun, the gun drill &c, the telephone by which we shall communicate, the work of an observation officer who watches the result of his battery's fire &c. Mervyn has started in lodging at Walthamstow & is cheerful about it. Bronwen is with an aunt a few miles from here. Baba is at Steep with the John Freemans who have our cottage there. Helen is walking with one of her sisters[3] up

---

[1] Thomas was now training as an officer cadet at the Royal Artillery school in Handel Street, London.

[2] I.e., an abscess.

in the Lake district. Meanwhile we are supposed to be moving to our new cottage in a week or two. I think there will be some delay. Helen runs away so comfortably from affairs, & I am not free to manage them now.

I see a few people now I am in barracks in London. Scott-James is a cadet with me. The Farjeons are not far off. Nor is Davies, but I never see him. Ellis & John Freeman I have seen. Garnett is still to see. We have missed one another a number of times since I enlisted.

I am likely to be at this preliminary training a month yet. It might only be 2 weeks but I am slow at it & likely not to go with the first batch to Wiltshire where we do more advanced work. I might get my commission next month. More likely it will be later. There is so much to learn & we are a big crowd with rather few instructors. Many of the men are more apt than I am—engineers, surveyors, schoolmasters &c. It is not like camp life. I make no friends. We are treated rather better & have fewer duties & responsibilities, fewer demands on one another, than in camp. The result is I am rather impatient to go out & be shot at. That is all I want, to do something if I am discovered to be any use, but in any case to be made to run risks, to be put through it. I have been saying to myself lately that I don't really care a fig what happens. But perhaps I do. —I am cut off. All the anchors are up. I have no friends now. Two I had in camp, but one is just going out to France & the other is still in camp & is not likely to come my way for some time; & both are 12 years younger than I am, & away from camp not likely to be so much like friends. I have a cold. I have no strength, so that beginning all over again comes harder.

I may go & see Haines some week end, but I don't feel equal to anything but idling here at my mother's for 24 hours at the weekends. My mother was operated on for cataract 6 weeks ago & they seem to think she will not get her sight back in that eye.

---

[3] Irene, who was lately a widow.

This is dismal reading. But I don't want money. Didn't I tell you the government had been persuaded to grant me £300? They would not give me a pension. That £300 might last till the end of the war. But those 50 faggots didn't. We took to cooking with them in the Summer out of doors & that spoilt my verses on the subject so far as they were a prophecy. It is no use me saying how much I wish I were destined to come & live at your farm. You know I think of it often. But of course the future is less explorable than usual & I don't take it (the future) quite seriously. I find myself thinking as if there wasn't going to be no future. This isn't perversity. I say I find myself doing so. On the other hand it may be I am just as wrong as when I wrote about those 50 faggots. I thought then that one simply had to wait a very long time. I wonder is it <u>pleasanter</u> to be Rupert Brookish. Anyhow it is impossible, & I suppose I enjoy this frame of mind as much as I can enjoy anything (beyond my dinner) at present.

Monday the 11th

This frame of mind is lasting too long. The fact is—my cold is worse & I am sick at not being really equal to my work. Once I get into the country I shall be all right.

I don't believe I can do much yet at 'The Old Cloak'. You can't imagine the degree of my disinclination for books. Sometimes I say I will read Shakespeare's Sonnets again & I do, or half do, but never more than that I should love to do it with you. I thought of what love poems could go in—could Burns's 'Whistle & I'll come to ye, my lad'? There are the songs in the very earliest Elizabethan dramatists. There's a deal of Chaucer, Shakespeare, Cowper, Wordsworth & the ballads: some Crabbe; one poem apiece out of Prior & several minor 18th century people: a few of Blake's. But I daren't begin to look at books: I must keep all my <u>conscious attention</u> for my work.

Mervyn looked none the worse yesterday for his 9 hours a day standing up in the factory. He is in lodgings till we make our move.

I have just been seeing off one of the 2 men I knew best at the Artists. He is just getting his commission & will be out long before me. I had some time to spare & called for Davies but he was out. He is only ½ a mile away. He is bringing out a big selection of his poems & looking for a great man to do an introduction.

A small new publisher I know is thinking of publishing my verses,[4] of course under the name of Edward Eastaway, & I believe 2 are to be included in an anthology of 'cheerful' poems at the Oxford press which Smith has a hand in.[5] He is in town but I haven't met him yet.

Goodbye & try to imagine me more like a soldier than this letter sounds. My love to you all & I hope Carol is much better.

Yours ever
Edward Thomas

Use this London address till you know the new one, not Steep any more.

---

[4] Roger Ingpen.

[5] This does not appear to have come off.

60. Frost to Thomas

Franconia N.H.
September 28 1916

Dear Edward:

I began to think our positions were reversed—you had got well-minded from having plunged into things and I had got soul-sick from having plunged out of them. Your letter shows you can still undertalk me when you like. A little vaccination and a little cold and you are down where it makes me dizzy to look in after you. You are so good at black talk that I believe your record will stand unbroken for years to come. It's as if somebody should do the hundred yards in five seconds flat.

But look at Lloyd George. You may be down-hearted, and I may be with you. But we have to admit that it is just as well to be able to say things and see things as courageously as he is. I say that quite for its face value. Lloyd George is one of the very great men. I wish I could expect my sins to be forgiven me as a Yankee, when I return to England, in the measure of my admiration for him. I'm afraid Englishmen aren't liking Americans very much just now. Should I dare to go back to England at this moment? I often long to. The hardest part of it would be to be treated badly for what is none of my fault personally.

Let's let the Old Cloak hang on the hat-tree till you put off soldier's uniform. Meanwhile I wish you could let me have copies of just the poems you are putting into book form. I am not a person of half the influence I should have thought I would be by this time. Nevertheless I must see what I can do to find you a publisher here and save you your copyright. I failed in a way that was no discredit to you with the Four and Twenty Blackbirds. "Too insular" was the praise our publishers damned it with for American purposes. I can see the way Henry Holt looked at it. And then it might have fared better if I could have thrust it upon him in book form—as I did The Listeners.[1] That might have helped the matter. I am making a clean breast of all this to give you a chance to refuse to let me see what I can do with the poems. You needn't feel obliged to humour me (as I do you in that spelling.) I sha'n't go to Holt this time; but to someone else who dropped in on me lately for a talk on what was doing in English writing. Never mind who it was for the present. Get up no hopes—as I know you are incapable of getting up any. Only let me try. It's a shame you shouldnt have something on someone's list over here where I find so many who know and like you. One of my professors at the University of Pennsylvania was liking the "perfect texture" of your prose just the other day—thought he had read all you had written. Mosher of Portland seemed to have a large knowledge of you. I'm not saying this to cheer you up, damn you. You know the worth of your bays. And I'm nobody to cheer anyone else when I can't cheer myself of late. And winte[r]s coming on.

I'm going to write you some all-fired stuff every week of my life.

Tell me, if you think of it, what your final opinion of Rupert's work is.

Our love. Always yours
Robert Frost

I wonder if there's the least chance of your being allowed to come over here on leave and say goodbye to us before you go out.[2]

---

[1] A book of poems by de la Mare.

[2] This sentence, clearly an afterthought, is written along the left margin of the first page of the letter.

61. Thomas to Frost

High Beech[1]
nr Loughton
19.x.16   *Essex.*

My dear Robert,

This morning the postman brought your letter of September 28.
I am at home helping to get things straight in our new cottage. It is
right alone in the forest among beech trees & fern & deer, though
it only costs 10^d. to reach London. Luckily I had a week's leave
thrust on me just at the time when I could be of some use. We have
had fine weather, too, luckily & have had some short walks, Helen,
Bronwen & I—Mervyn being still in lodgings 6 miles off, & Baba
with an aunt, waiting till the house is ready for them.

Since I wrote last I have been shifted to Trowbridge Artillery
Barracks & have had 3 weeks hard work there. I am waiting for the
result of my 2nd examination. If I pass, I shall be an officer in an-
other month. My going out depends on whether they are in great
need of men when I am ready, also on my passing the final medical
test. If I go it seems likely it will be to a not very big gun, so that I
shall be far enough up to see everything. There may be a week's
leave before that, there may not, in any case not enough to come to
see you even if that were allowed, which I doubt. If you were to
come over here I don't think you would meet much annoyance, if
any. People say things you would not like to hear, but the chances

---

[1] Where the Thomases had their new cottage. They moved toward the end of September.

are a hundred to one you would not hear them. There is certainly no strong feeling. What feeling there is only unlucky chance or your own putting it to the test could bring out. I don't like to think of your coming & my not being free to see you. I have short week ends of 24 hours—giving me less than 24 hours at home. In a month's time I may have a number of days of freedom, but I can count on nothing.

I have just written the 2nd thing since I left London a month ago.[2] If I can type the 2 you shall see them. I am wondering if any of these last few sets of verses have pleased you at all. —Haines liked some I showed him. I was there for 24 hours a fortnight ago & had a walk up Cooper's Hill & picked blueberries. He was the same as ever, & relieved at his (apparently final) exemption. I think he was going to write to you then. He showed me Hyla Brook & another piece of yours which I enjoyed very much. I like nearly everything of yours better at a 2nd reading & best after that. True.

About my collection of verses, the publisher remains silent a month. I wrote off at once today to ask whether he could decide & if he will publish I will do my best to hunt up duplicates & send them out to you in good time for a possible American publisher. I shall be pleased if you succeed & not feel it a scrap if you don't. As if I could refuse to give you a chance of doing me good!

It would take me too long to be sure what I think of Rupert. I can tell you this—that I received £3 for his first 'Poems' the other day & £2 for 'New Numbers' (because of him). So I can't think entirely ill of him. No, I don't think ill of him. I think he succeeded in being youthful & yet intelligible & interesting (not only pathologically) more than most poets since Shelley. But thought gave him (and me) indigestion. He couldn't mix his thought or the result of it with his feeling. He could only think about his feeling. Radically, I think he lacked power of expression. He was a rhetorician, dress-

---

[2] Probably "The Child in the Orchard." The other poem, after leaving London, may have been "The Trumpet."

ing things up better than they needed. And I suspect he knew too well both what he was after & what he achieves. I think perhaps a man ought to be capable of always being surprised on being confronted with what he really is—as I am nowadays when I confront a full size mirror in a good light instead of a cracked bit of one in a dark barrack room. Scores of men, by the way, shave outside the window, just looking at the glass with the dawn behind them. My disguises increase, what with spurs on my heels & hair on my upper lip.

Bronwen is at my elbow reading 'A Girl of the Limberlost'. Garnett, whom I saw yesterday, for the first time since I enlisted, was praising 'The Spoon River Anthology'.[3] Can he be right? I only glanced at it once, & I concluded that it must be liked for the things <u>written about</u> in it, not for what it expressed. Isn't it done too much on purpose?

Noyes is reciting to the public, not to a drawing room. He was too valuable to be made a soldier. Monro has gone off to camp somewhere, but not so Miss . . . . . . arski[.][4]

You would like one of our sergeant-major instructors who asked a man coiling a rope the wrong way—from right to left—'Were you a snake-charmer before you joined'. We have some ripe regular specimens at the barracks. By the way, have you had any news of Chandler? I asked Haines, but he didn't know. Flint, I suppose, has been gathered up by now.

Now I will try to type those verses. Goodbye. Helen & Bronwen & I send you all our love. Bronwen, by the way, wrote to Irma in August, addressing her at Bethlehem. I wonder with what luck.

Yours ever

Edward Thomas

---

[3] By Edgar Lee Masters, published in 1915.

[4] Kzementarski.

62. Thomas to Frost

4 xi 16   *Trowbridge*[1]

My dear Robert

This is just in case I don't have as good a chance of writing a letter next week. It is the eve of another examination—I scraped through the first—and there is a lull in the work. If I get through I shall have only another week here then a week of field work nearby, then after some leave to buy clothes &c we finish up with 2 or 3 weeks practical experience; but before that last term I should be an officer. Beyond that I shan't know anything for some time. The cinematograph pictures of the 'Somme Battle' tell you exactly nothing. I went to see them last night. You can learn far more from two or three soldiers talking about women.

Your letter with the 2 photographs & the advertisement of 'Successful Americans' came this week. As soon as I know what the publisher means to do I will send you duplicates. I have them ready, but he doesn't intend to publish them all, so I must wait. He wants my name to appear, & I don't. It is to be Edward Eastaway. I hope you will not object.

I was home for a few hours last week & saw all the children again. They were all very well. Mervyn talks a good deal more, & what we can see is all improvement. They like the new house & its position, though I don't know whether Helen will enjoy the solitude especially if a Zeppelin comes near, as it often does. We see deer in

---

[1] At firing camp.

the road frequently & hear them now. We can pick up all our fire wood 200 yards off. Helen's Leghorns have just begun to lay. The worst yet is we must use a lot of wire netting if we grow anything that rabbits like. The expense has made a difference, but with Mervyn earning about 5/- a week & Bronwen at a cheaper school we ought to recover from the move in a year.

De la Mare sails for America tomorrow & I hope you will see him. It is some time since I saw him. We rather fence with one another now, remembering we once got on very well.

I am expecting news from Freeman (not John Freeman the bard) who has just had to join the army & had no idea what was to happen to him. He was passed for Garrison Duty abroad.

Edward Garnett is sending some of my verses to the 'Nation'. Eleanor Farjeon tries them sometimes with my things but always in vain.[2]

We have 3 afternoons for exercise now & we (4 or 5 of us) usually run & walk for a couple of hours, I leading as I know the ground. It is a good way of enjoying the bad weather. One day when the sun was warm we bathed in the Frome. This is the country I came to when I wrote my 'Swinburne'.[3] It has two good little rivers, one in a shallow level valley, the other in a steepsided narrow one. There is a castle & many fine old houses near, & Salisbury Main just too far off for our short afternoons, but its old White House plainly visible all day.

Goodbye. I shall write again soon if I can. My love to you all.

Yours ever
Edward Thomas

---

[2] Eleanor Farjeon had acted as a kind of agent/secretary for Thomas, in connection with his poetry, since shortly after he began composing. Poems sent out to publishers were sent from her residence so as to preserve the secret identity of "Eastaway."

[3] *Swinburne: A Critical Study* (1912).

63. Frost to Thomas

Dear Edward:

Tomorrow we vote—I vote for once; and you mustn't be disappointed if we don't turn Wilson out of office. We probably shall turn him out from a mistaken idea of what we are about. But don't be disappointed if we don't. By comparison with a number of Americans I could name he has been a real friend of the Allies' cause. Roosevelt is the only man we have who could have lead us into war with the Germans. And he would have had to betray us into it. It would have had to be almost betrayal; because though we are very much on your side, we seem to have no general wish to be in the fighting. You will see how it will be with Hughes if he is elected. He will set himself simply to beat Wilson at his own game. Granting that Wilson has given us a good deal of peace with some honour, Hughes' aim will be to give us more peace with more honour— especially the more honour. He's a confident fool who thinks he sees how it will be easy to do this. He is one of those Sunday School products who is going to be every bit as good as he has brains to be. None of him for me.

And yet you know how I feel about the war. I have stopped as-severating from a sense of fitness. You rather shut me up by enlisting. Talk is almost too cheap when all your friends are facing bullets. I don't believe I ought to enlist (since I am of course an American), but if I can't enlist, at least I refuse to talk sympathy beyond a certain point. I did set myself to wish this country into the war. I made a little noise on the subject, but soon found I wasn't half as good at the noise as some who cared less. (Has Harold Begbie enlisted?) When all the world is facing danger, it's a shame not to be facing danger for any reason, old age, sickness, or any other. Words wont make the shame less. There's no use trying to make out that the shame we suffer makes up for the more heroic things we don't suffer. No more of this for a long time. Are not the magazines chuckfull of it?

I hear from a friend of mine who if he doesnt love the Germans as against the British at least loves the Irish as against them, that De la Mare is to dine or lunch or something with him when he gets to New York. The time named is so near that I guess De la Mare isn't going to make me a port of call or he would have got some word to me before this. Is it that he doesn't know that you and Garnett and he and Abercrombie and one or two others have made me even more distinguished than he is in this country. I'm a little hurt. Of course we are a little out of the way. Masefield wrote that he meant to get out here (uninvited), but his agent rushed him off his feet up to the last moment of his stay and he couldnt make it. Very likely Masefield wanted to see my Dominique (pronounced Dominik) hens.

Is there the least use in beseeching you to come over for a week or two out of my pocket? Could you get leave? I wish it beyond anything. I should think it ought to be possible. We could find you a few lectures. Taking the fast boats you ought not to have to be gone more than three weeks. Does this sound so very unmilitary? They ought to consider that you were literary before you were military. I have a play I shall be half afraid of till you tell me how it strikes you. Its the same old one I tried to make you read once before when I first knew you—if you remember—and you sidestepped it. It is called An Assumed Part.

I (personally) am in what is known as an "interesting state". I may have news for you in my next letter. Oh, by the way, I came across my Gibsonian lines On Being about to Become a Parent just lately. Now don't misunderstand me. There are other offspring than of our bodies.

Farewell and adieu to you with a fa la la la la la la, and don't forget your old shipmate

Robert Frost, the Frisco-Digger, Boston Beauty, etc.

64. Thomas to Frost

High Beech
Loughton
Essex

24 xi 16.

My dear Robert,

As soon as I got back from Bottomley's, where I spent two whole days & 3 nights, I found your letter & Elinor's. We could not help smiling that you should think it possible I could come over to America. In any case I might very well be in France before Christmas. I hope so. At least I should prefer not to have a Christmas in England just before going out. I want to go soon, to get over the first & worst step (of parting). Even the leave I have got now is not quite satisfactory. I can't think of enjoying it quite. Yet I did enjoy being up at Bottomley's. We often talked of you. I inquired for the poems you are giving to the Annual, but they were not there. When we got on to 'Poetry'[1] he suggested my sending there the things which are to appear in the 'Annual'. Here they are. I thought you would not mind sending them on as from Edward Eastaway—they said something agreeable about 'Lob' in their notes some months ago.

You must not take it at all badly if de la Mare does not come. Probably he would if you asked him. But he does not often go anywhere when he is not actually asked. He will be anxious & uneasy in America. He did not want to go & people will be crowd-

---

[1] The poetry journal edited by Harriet Monroe.

ing round him. If he found himself in your house I imagine he would be as glad as you. I hope he will come. I hear he may stay till February, tho he did speak of coming back for Christmas.

My book will soon be decided on & then I shall send you duplicates. These things I send now are all exclusive to the Annual.

Please thank Elinor & tell her not to think of me as in poor health. I have never found what I have had to do too much for me. In the future the worst I shall have to suffer (apart from injury) will be cold & excitement, & I shall be better able to support things when I have no excuse for considering myself or my feelings. I think I can be a much more useful person than you would imagine from seeing me amidst ease & comfort. I shall write wherever I go. Probably I shall write before I go out, as that can hardly be for another 3 or 4 weeks.

Goodbye. My love to Elinor & the children.

Yours ever
Edward Thomas

PS. You can count on the Annual not appearing before February, I think. I shall not be a 2nd Lieutenant till next week. And when I am you address me as usual, except when writing to me at my Battery & I don't know that yet[.]

65. Thomas to Elinor Frost

High Beech
27 xi 16   *Loughton Essex*

My dear Elinor,

Thank you for your letter. There are two things I want to do, to go out & to come & see you. I hope I shall do them both. But I confess I think chiefly of the first now, as of the beginning of a day. The other would be like arriving in the evening & I can't quite think of that. When the time comes I shall. Robert's photograph arrived late last week. It had been forwarded to Bottomley's or I should have had it before. It seems to me & all of us excellent. Baba liked the knot in the wood of the deck particularly. The photograph set us all imagining. I am very glad to have it. I would send you one of myself on the same scale if anyone would come round here to take it. I don't like going out to be photographed in my fine clothes. They are too fine & new. I don't know how I shall feel when they are older. Meantime Mervyn will have a shot at me.

I am still on leave, waiting for a telegram. It is an interval I am not going to enjoy as much as I fancied. But I have been busy too, correcting the proofs of my poems that are to appear with Robert's in Trevelyan's annual, also in arranging the MS. for my book. The duplicate shall be sent to Robert in a day or two. Please tell him no time has been fixed for publication, but I suppose it might be early next year & I don't at all expect he will be able to arrange anything in time. If he wants to know my publishers they are Selwyn & Blount, but the person to deal with is

Roger Ingpen
28 Queen Anne's Grove
Bedford Park
London W.

I believe he is both Selwyn & Blount. You will not be surprised to see Robert's name connected with them.

Haines has just written to tell me of a long poem by Robert he has just read somewhere: he foolishly does not send it.[1]

We like our new home. Except Saturdays & Sundays & holidays we see only aeroplanes & deer in the forest. Baba has no companions. She goes about telling herself stories. She is a sensitive selfish little creature. Helen has only her, so I suppose she must be spoilt. The others are really only at home to sleep except at week end. The forest is beautiful, oaks, hornbeams, beeches, bracken, hollies, & some heather. But it is really High Beach not Beech, on account of the pebbly soil. There are 7 or 8 miles of forest, by 1 or 2 miles wide, all on the high ground, with many tiny ponds & long wide glades. We have few neighbors & know none of them yet. But it is easy for people to get here from London. We are half an hour from the station which is half an hour from the city. Helen is going to find it lonely. She does not stand these times very well. If she did, I should have really nothing at all to worry about.

But I have gone & caught a chill, & I don't feel like talking at all. Goodbye. My love to Robert & the children.

Ever yours
Edward Thomas

---

[1] Probably "Snow," published in *Poetry* for November.

66. Thomas to Frost

High Beech
nr Loughton
Essex

29 xi 16

My dear Robert,

I just arranged this book[1] in the nick of time. For a letter came today warning me to expect a call to my 'new unit'. Which means probably going straight to a battery & not to any final school. Not that I have learnt everything. I simply can't master the field artillery telephone. But then I have practically never seen it yet! I have only just seen the gun I am going to. I suppose I ought not to tell you what it is. I understand it will be about 1500 yards behind the front line trenches, so that I shall see a great deal. I was gazetted last Friday. That is to say I am now 2nd. Lieutenant.

So how can I see your play? It did make us all smile to think you thought I might come over for a week. It is one of the impossiblest things. I wish I had not sidestepped it. I remember I did when I was impatient to get on with that novel. You had your revenge, though: you prepared a precipice instead of a step & the wretched thing fell over & there it is at the bottom still. One of the things I have to thank you for. I hope I shall still see the play. A copy typed might be a blessing if this winter over there is at all dull at intervals. I expect you had better always address me here as perhaps the number of the Siege Battery I am going to would

---

[1] A duplicate of the Eastaway MS was sent with this letter.

be exceptionable.[2] 'Siege artillery' is a very special but not descriptive term which you can conclude nothing from.

We are having fine cold days. I have had a chill, spent a wretched day in bed, had got over it in order to go to my tailor's. I wish you could come shopping with me. I never spent so much in a week. Clothes! And I always preferred clothes old & loose & now they are all new & close fitting. Perhaps Mervyn will photograph me in them, but I really can't go to the west end & do it.

Eleanor Farjeon is here now & she & Helen &[3] marking my clothes.

Mervyn goes off at a quarter to seven every morning. He has to cycle 7 miles to his work while the owls & the deer are still about the roads. All day we hear a noise in one of the big munition factories, just like a huge woodpecker tapping in the forest—about 7 or 8 rapid declining taps. Aeroplanes are really the commonest big birds over the forest.

There was a mystery in your last letter. Let me know when the event takes place & what it is.

The book is to be simply 'Poems' unless the publisher prefers 'Lob & other Poems' or 'The Trumpet & other Poems'.

Now goodbye. I won't keep this till I have more news, but write again if possible.

Yours ever
Edward Thomas.

---

[2] To the censor.

[3] For *are*.

67. Frost to Thomas

Franconia N.H.
December 7 1916

Dear Edward:

I have been down sick in bed for a week and a half: thats where I have been and thats why you haven't heard from me. Port wine is what I need now if I am going to shine. But I'm not. I find that the chief thing on my mind is not a personal one, whats going to become of you and me—nothing like that—but a political one[:] the change in the government in England and the possibilities of great changes in France. What becomes of my hopes of three months ago when the drive on the Somme began? Something has gone wrong. How can we be happy any more—for a while. Lloyd George is the great man and he belongs where he now takes his place. But would he ever have arrived there with Bonar Law and Carson on his right and left, but for some desperate need. Silly fools are full of peace talk over here. It is out of friendliness of a kind to the Allies: they act as if they thought you were waiting for them to say the word to quit. It's none of my business what you do: but neither is it any of theirs. I wrote some lines I've copied on the other side of this about the way I am struck. When I get to writing in this vein you may know I am sick or sad or something.

Robert

Suggested by Talk of Peace at This Time[1]

France, France, I know not what is in my heart.
But God forbid that I should be more brave
As watcher from a quiet place apart
Than you are fighting in an open grave.

I will not ask more of you than you ask,
O Bravest, of yourself. But shall I less?
You know the extent of your appointed task,
Whether you still can face its bloodiness.

Not mine to say you shall not think of peace.
Not mine, not mine. I almost know your pain.
But I will not believe that you will cease,
I will not bid you cease, from being slain

And slaying till what might have been distorted
Is saved to be the Truth and Hell is thwarted.

R.F.

---

[1] Not published by Frost. Printed in *CPPP* as "On Talk of Peace at this Time," with many variants.

68. Thomas to Frost

16 xii 16.

My dear Robert,

   I am not really at home but am beginning my third week at a big artillery training camp.[1] Leave has practically ceased & I hardly expect to go home again till just before I go out to France. That is now likely to be in January. I don't think before that. I have only today been posted to a battery. My first job—all the other officers being away—was to give a man leave to see his wife die in Birmingham. It was hard to be as judicial as an officer is expected to be.

   Well, now I can assume I have put away childish things & am about to work. The past fortnight has been just a rapid resumé of what I have done in the past 3 or 4 months. It ended with an examination in which, as usual, I was nearer the bottom than the top, with 77%. I think I know all I shall ever learn from lectures & books. The rest will all be practical work & I think I can go ahead a little faster.

   There isn't much I can say now. I haven't got over the time of waiting in uncertainty to know whether I was to go straight over or to stay here a little longer to train with a battery. I have to get

---

[1] Royal Garrison Artillery, Lydd, Kent.

over the annoyance, too, of remaining in England over Christmas & not going home.

No news. The book is not quite fixed up. One or two pieces may have to be cut out to make it the right length.

I hear de la Mare is out and busy.

This is nothing to send but in case I don't write anything more interesting I shall post it. With my love to you all.

Yours ever
Edward Thomas.

I forgot to mention that in my squad before I came here was a young Bostonian, named Gibson, who had an English mother & elected to come over here to fight.

69. Thomas to Frost

31 xii 1916.   *High Beech*

My dear Robert,

I had your letter & your poem 'France, France' yesterday. I like the poem very much, because it betrays exactly what you *would* say & what you feel about saying that much. It expresses just those hesitations you or I would have at asking others to act as we think it is their cue to act. Well, I am soon going to know more about it. I am not at home as the address suggests, but am on the eve of a whole week's continuous shooting. It begins tomorrow. Then at the end of the week or soon after I shall have my last leave. After all we are going to have smaller guns than we thought & we shall be nearer the front lines a good bit & are beginning to make insincere jokes about observing from the front line which of course we shall have to do. I think I told you we were a queer mixed crowd of officers in this battery. As soon as we begin to depend on one another we shall no doubt make the best of one another. I am getting on, I think, better than when I was in my pupilage. The 2 senior officers have been out before. Four of us are new. I am 3 years older than the commanding officer & twice as old as the youngest. I mustn't say much more.

I was home for Christmas by an unexpected piece of luck. We were very happy with housework & wood gathering in the forest & a few walks. We had snow & sunshine on Christmas day. Mervyn's holiday coincided with mine. Some of the time I spent at my mother's house & in London buying the remainder of my things for the front. I am very well provided.

I wish I had your book.[1] Haines has, but I don't want to borrow his. Mine still hasn't been fixed up. I wonder have you had your duplicate of the M.S. which I sent over a month ago? It looks now as if I should not see the proofs. Bottomley or John Freeman will do it for me.

It is nearly all work here now & in the evenings, if I haven't something to do with my maps for next day, I am either out walking or indoors talking. When I am alone—as I am during the evening just now because the officer who shares my room is away— I hardly know what to do. I can't write now & still less can I read. I have rhymed but I have burnt my rhymes & feel proud of it. Only on Saturday & Sunday have we a chance of walking in daylight. Twice I have seen Conrad who lives 12 miles away. But now we can't travel by train without special reasons. I tried to begin 'The Shaving of Shagpat'[2] just now, but could not get past the 3rd page. I could read Frost, I think. Send me another letter, though I expect it will find me over the sea. Goodbye all, & my love.

Yours ever
Edward Thomas.

---

[1] *Mountain Interval*, published November 1916.

[2] By George Meredith.

IV. 1917 and After

70. Thomas to Frost

12 i 17   *England*

My dear Robert,

I have just had my last leave. We are warned for foreign service & I expect I shall be in France when this reaches you. We have done our shooting. I enjoyed the actual work at the guns & the observing. Now I am rather impatient to go I have said the last of my farewells except this. I shall write to you out there as much as I can. You will be seeing Gibson possibly. He has stolen a march on me. But I suppose you may be interning him yet. I should not like that. But I may have worse things to dislike. I am quite well & in good spirits except when I think of Helen. I doubt if she is very strong to bear what she has to bear. Mervyn will be attesting on Monday, his 17th birthday. He will not be liable for service for a year. If there is still war then he will try for the Flying Corps.

I saw my publisher a day or two ago. He says he thinks he can publish the verses whole as I sent them to you & he will wait a while in case he hears from you, which I don't expect. Perhaps you never had them or the earlier batch I sent you. In any case I dare not hope you can have time to arrange anything even if you have a willing publisher.

Davies said a Davies-like thing when I saw him 2 days ago. We were talking of Trevelyan's Annual. He said he had only 5 short things in it—'probably the smallest contribution—in bulk'.

I wonder have you seen de la Mare?

My love to Elinor & all of you.

Yours ever
Edward Thomas.

71. Thomas to Frost

still England

22 i 17

My dear Robert,

I could take a day off so I went to see Haines. I couldn't go &
see Helen or my mother. You understand. I said goodbye 10 days
ago. We move any day this week, & I will keep this by me till I
know for certain where I will be. Haines gave me a spare copy of
'Mountain Interval' he had, & I have read everything except 'Snow'.
I am not going to put them in order of liking, because I couldn't.
I did admire, but much more it was getting close to you again that
the reading meant. Probably it is that makes me more homesick
than I have been for some time. Homesick or something. 'The
Home Stretch' by itself would be enough. I shall be able to take
the book out with me to France now.

Mervyn attested on Saturday but will be free to go on with his
work for almost another year. If he has to leave he would choose
the Flying Corps, he says.

You have borrowed Gibson from us. Pray don't trouble to re-
turn him unless empty.

I can ride a motor cycle now. (Reporting progress is about all I
can do towards a letter.) But I daresay such things don't make much
difference. You hear girls in trains saying that 'facing realities' will
change so-and-so (& of course improve him): as if 'realities' hadn't
always been as common as mud. So-and-so can't face more than
he was born to, I expect: nor I. So that I worry less & less about

that gamekeeper. Old Haines has got exemption till June 30 now & is naturally relieved—to <u>have</u> to go so late must be distressing. We didn't walk at all. I had one night there, & we just sat up talking & smoking.

I have had some walks over the Downs & revisited several places—in the intervals of work. Twice too I had to march the battery along the roads I used to travel on my way up to Ledington. We have been having nice hard clean weather luckily, for we are in a place renowned for mud, not country mud either, nor town mud—where there used to be 1000 people now there are 100 000 & you have now[1] idea how decivilising this life is in some ways—or rather how thin it shows our civil[i]zation to be.

Later

We are off on the 28th and 29th.[2] I have had rather little to do these two days & have had sore ankles from a new pair of boots, so that I am thinking that anything will be better than hanging about. But I daresay it isn't so. It is always a part of this life to have to hang about in cold & wet & then not to have a minute to spare. Anyhow it is always better to do a thing than to 'imagine' what it would be like to do it. Someday we can discuss the difference—that is if you have imagined [it] at all.

Goodbye. I wish the post would bring a letter from you before I go. My love to you all.

Yours ever
Edward Thomas

---

[1] For *no*.

[2] I.e., to France.

72. Frost to Helen Thomas

Amherst Mass[1]
February 6 1917

My dear Helen:

I am writing this to you because I think it may be the quickest way to reach Edward with questions I must have an answer to as soon as possible.

I have found a publisher for his poems in America. But there are several things to be cleared up before we can go ahead.

Has Edward sold the 'world' rights to his English publisher or only the English rights? That is to say is he free to deal directly with an American publisher?

Dont you think he ought to throw off the pen-name and use his real name under the circumstances? Shall we make him? Tell him I insist.

Would he object very much if I took it into my head at the publishers suggestion to write a little preface to the book to take the place of the dedication?[2]

I am not going to ask permission to take up with the offer of ten percent royalty. Any royalty is all right. The thing is to get the poems out where they may be read.

---

[1] The Frosts moved from Franconia to Amherst late in January, when Robert accepted an offer of a professorship from Amherst College.

[2] The English edition of the book was dedicated "To Robert Frost." The preface was never written.

My hope is that Edward hasn't lost the right to let us set the book up over here.

I have just sold two or three of the poems to Harriet Monroe of Poetry, Chicago.[3] The money will have to come to me and so to you unless we decide at once to use real names.

Isn't this rather pleasant news for the soldier?—damn his eyes.

I am a teacher again for the moment and we are all here at Amherst, Mass, the town of my college.

I wonder if it would be too much trouble for Merfyn to write a pretty little note to Frederick Howe, Commissioner of Immigration, Ellis Island New York to thank him for the glimpse he gave him of these United States and to tell him that he is safely back in his own country and promised as a soldier when his country shall want him? I have meant to ask Merfyn myself. I had a nice letter from him awhile ago.

I doubt if his country is going to need him. I suspect that all that is happening is some ingenuity of the Germans to bring the war to an early close without having to seem beaten. I don't know just what they are up to. I think, though, they are looking for a way to let go of the Lion's tail. I begin to think we shall be seeing you all again before long.

Always yours
Robert

---

[3] "Old Man," "The Word," and "The Unknown" appeared in the February 1917 issue of Poetry.

73. Thomas to Frost

Feb. 11 & a Sunday they tell me.

My dear Robert,

I left England a fortnight ago & have now crawled with the battery up to our position. I can't tell you where it is, but we are well up in high open country. We are on a great main road in a farmhouse facing the enemy who are about 2 miles away, so that their shells rattle our windows but so far only fall a little behind us or to one side. It is near the end of a three weeks frost. The country is covered with snow which silences everything but the guns. We have slept chiefly in uncomfortable places till now. Here we lack nothing except letters from home. It takes some time before a new unit begins to receive its letters. I have enjoyed it very nearly all, except shaving in a freezing tent. I don't think I really knew what travel was like till we left England.

Yesterday, our second day, I spent in the trenches examining observation posts to see what could be seen of the enemy from them. It was really the best day I have had since I began. We had some shells very near us, but were not sniped at. I could see the German lines very clear, but not a movement anywhere, nothing but posts sticking out of the snow with barbed wire, bare trees broken & dead & half ruined houses. The only living men we met at bends in the trenches eating or carrying food or smoking. One dead man lay under a railway arch so stiff & neat (with a covering of sacking) that I only slowly realised he was dead. I got back tired & warm & red. I hope I shall never enjoy anything less. But I shall. Times are comparatively quiet just here. We shall be busy soon & we shall not be alone. I am now just off with a working party to prepare our gun positions which are at the edge of a cathedral town a mile or less along the road we took out on. We are to fight in an orchard there in sight of the cathedral.

It is night & cold again. Machine guns rattle & guns go 'crump' in front of us. Inside, a gramophone plays the rottenest songs imaginable, jaunty unreal dirty things. We get on well enough but we six are a rum company. There is a Scotch philosopher, an impossible unmilitary creature who looks far more dismal than he really can be[.] —I like him to talk to, but he is too gloomy timid & apologetic & helpless to live with. The others are all commonplace people under 26 years old who are never serious & could not endure anyone else serious. We just have to be dirty together. I also cannot be sincere with them. Two are boys of 19 & make me think of the boys I might have had for company. One of the two aged about 24 is rather a fine specimen of the old English soldiers, always bright and smart and capable, crude but goodhearted & frivolous & yet thorough at their work. He has been 10 years in the army. All his talk is in sort of proverbs or cant sayings & bits of comic songs, coarse metaphors—practically all quotation.

But I am seldom really tired of them so I suppose I am jilting at who they are, & their lack of seriousness is no deception & is just their method of expression.

I used to read some of the Sonnets[1] while we were at Havre, but not in these last few days of travel. 'Mountain Interval' also is waiting.

My love to you all,
Yours ever
(2/Lt) Edward Thomas
244 Siege Battery
B.E.F. France

---

[1] Thomas had a copy of Shakespeare's *Sonnets* with him.

74. Thomas to Frost
Feb 23

My dear Robert,

It is going to be harder than ever for us to talk, I suppose. I did write you a week or so back after I first went & had a look round in the trenches. I had my first letter from home soon after & Helen said she had heard from Elinor but did not enclose the letter. Well, I have read "Snow" today & that puts me on to you. I liked it. You go in for 'not too much' in a different sense from Horace's & yet your 'not too much' is just as necessary. But I can't read much. I am temporarily thrust out of my Battery to assist in some head-quarters work with maps &c. We are living in rather a palace—a very cold dark palace—about 2000 yards from the Hun, in a city which is more than half in ruins already. It is full of our men & no doubt one night we shall know that the Hun knows it. I woke last night thinking I heard someone knocking excitedly at a door nearby. But I am persuaded now it was only a machine gun. My battery is not doing much but digging. The weather is wet, dull & cold after the frost & it is impossible to shoot much. But I am very anxious to go back soon to my battery. They are only 3 miles away & when I walk over to see them it is something like going home. I am in a way at home there but here I have a Heavy Artillery Group Commander to hang about after & do as he pleases & my soul is less my own. You know that life is in so strange that I am only half myself & the half that knows England & you is obediently asleep for a time. Do you believe me? It seems that I have sent it to sleep to make the life endurable—more than endurable, really enjoyable in a way. But with the people I meet I am suppressing practically everything (without difficulty tho not without pain). I reserve all criticism just as I reserve all description. If I come back I shall boast of the book I did not write in this ruined city. Helen will tell you what city it is. I daren't tell a neutral more than that it is a small cathedral city. It is beautiful chalk country all round. What puzzles me is that I haven't heard a thrush sing yet, & of course not a blackbird.

Do write when you can to 244 Siege Battery, B.E.F., France, if only because I am probably the only man in A who has read "Mountain Interval'. My love to you all.

Yours ever
Edward Thomas

75. Thomas to Frost

March 6

My dear Robert

I still don't hear from you, but I had better write when I can. One never knows. I have now been living 2 weeks in a city that is only 2400 yds from the enemy, is shelled every day & night & is likely to be heavily bombarded some day. Of course the number of shells that fall is larger than the number of casualties although the place is crowded & falling masonry helps the shells, but this does not really appeal to anything but the brains that may be knocked out by them. Nor is it consoling to know that the enemy has put shells into the orchard where the battery is & all round it without injuring anybody. However it may console those who are not out here.

For these 2 weeks I have been detached from my battery to work at headquarters, which has meant getting to know something of how battle is conducted, & also going about with maps & visiting observation posts, some of which give a view of No Man's Land like a broad river very clear & close. We went out yesterday morning to see the Gordons cross to raid the enemy but it was snowing & we only saw snow & something moving & countless shell bursts beyond. Our artillery made a roof over our heads of shells ringing & shuffling along in shoals. —I return to the battery, a mile away, very soon now.

We are having many fine days, bright & warm even at times, & we begin to see larks as well as aeroplanes. I wish we did not see so many of the enemy's. Every clear day we are continually hearing the whistle blowing the alarm. It concerns the artillery very much as the planes spot us & then tell their batteries how to hit us.

I have not a great deal to do as a rule. Long hours of waiting, nothing that has to be done & yet not free to do what I want, in fact not consciously wanting anything except, I suppose, the end. Wisdom perhaps trickles in, perhaps not. There is nobody I like much, that is the worst of it. I don't want friends. I don't think I should like to have friends out here. I am sure I shouldn't. But I want companions & I hardly expect to find them. This may not be final. There are plenty of likable people. There is also one very intelligent man here, the signalling officer, an architect before the war, a hard clever pungent fellow who knows the New Age, Georgian Poetry (& doesn't like it) &c. He didn't seem to know 'Mountain Interval' or the author.

A letter from de la Mare came yesterday. So he has seen you. He says you don't look as well as you ought to. Whatever he said would be little or nothing, so I need not complain that he said nothing. He said he wished we could have a talk. Fancy being polite to me out here. Well, there is nothing I want to forget so far. Is that right?

I have time to spare but I can't talk. You don't answer, & I am inhibiting introspection except when I wake up & hear the shelling & wonder whether I ought to move my bed away from the window to the inner side where there is more masonry—more to resist & more to fall on me. But it is no use thinking like this. I am half awake when I do. Besides I have hardly learnt yet to distinguish between shells going out & shells coming in—my worst alarm was really shells going out. So far it excites but doesn't disturb, or at any rate doesn't upset & unfit.

I hear my book is coming out soon. Did the duplicate verses ever reach you? You have never said so. But don't think I mind. I should like to be a poet, just as I should like to live, but I know as much about my chances in either case, & I don't really trouble about either. Only I want to come back more or less complete. Goodbye. My dearest love to you all.

Yours ever
Edward Thomas.

76. Thomas to Frost

March 8

My dear Robert,

So you did find a publisher after all. I have just heard. Probably it is too late, but I can do nothing, & I must stick to Edward Eastaway. It would be absurd to call myself one thing here & one thing in America & here it is settled. I don't want to change. I can't think about it now but I just feel stubborn on that point.

How glad I was to see your writing—I was interrupted to send for a despatch rider. But now as I have to sit up for his return alone I can write a little & keep myself awake with some claret & hot water. You see we live in some luxury. As a matter of fact the city itself provides nothing but necessities but occasionally a car goes back 20 miles & brings up anything you like to pay for, & this mess pays for wine. I told you, I think, that I was temporarily at the headquarters of Heavy Artillery Group which is not in the snug safe place you expect headquarters to be in. Thank goodness I leave here tomorrow & return to more strenuous & more absorbing work. I will have plenty of nights up henceforward.

You sound more hopeful than most people are here. Not that they are despondent, but that they just don't know what to think. They know that the newspapers are stupid & the Hun wise; & there practically is the end of their knowledge. We are still fairly quiet here except for brief raids on the enemy. I went out to see one at breakfast time the other morning. The place I went to gave ordinarily a perfect view of the ground to be fought over but I saw in fact only snow & heard the artillery. But I told you this before, I believe.

We had still more snow today & I enjoyed being out in it just as 2 days before I enjoyed the warm sun & the clear sky with almost as many birds as aeroplanes in the sky. Yesterday was cold & raw & I became very depressed & solitary by the evening. Very soon, I expect to have no time or room left for depression.

I know some things about houses now that you don't know. The houses I observe from, for example, are all modern small houses, the last left standing before you come to the front line trenches. In front of them no houses for about 1500 yards, that is to say about the same distance behind the enemy as we are behind our troops. No Man's Land is 150 yards wide. These modern houses have all been hit & downstairs is a mixture of bricks mortar bedsteads & filth. Upstairs you spy out through tiles at the enemy, who knows perfectly well you are in one of these houses & someday will batter them all down. One of the houses is at the edge of a suburb of the city. One is at the edge of a pretty old village. It was being finished when war overtook it. If a shell hits it it will fall all to pieces, not in huge masses of masonry like the old brickwork at the citadel. But it is not so much individual houses as streets. You can't paint death living in them. —As I went to the village house today I heard a very young child talking in another equally exposed house in the same street. Some are too poor or too helpless or what to leave even these places. But I probably am not going to describe any more except to make a living.

What is Harriet going to do to maintain my family?[1] That was very good news. The money is the thing.

I already know enough to confirm my old opinion that the papers tell no truth at all about what war is & what soldiers are—except that they do play football close to the fighting line & play instruments of brass too—here we often hear the bagpipes.

When is that despatch rider coming back? He has 9 miles to do on a straight moonlit road that the enemy usually leaves alone for

---

[1] Harriet Monroe. I.e., in payment for the poems Frost sold to her.

some reason, though it is a main & crowded artery. Why is he so economical? I don't believe it is pure poverty. ——

Here he comes & I will shut this up & post it tomorrow, that is on March 9th.

77. Thomas to Frost
April 2

My dear Robert,

Hearing that the mails have been lost several times lately at sea I thought I had better make another shot at you. This is another penultimate letter. Things are closely impending now & will have happened before you get this & you will know all about them, so I will not try to tell you what they are, especially as I could not get them past the censor.

I have seen some new things since I wrote last & had mud & worse things to endure which do not become less terrible in anticipation but are less terrible once I am in the midst of them. Jagged gables at dawn when you are cold & tired out look a thousand times worse from their connection with a certain kind of enemy shell that has made them look like that, so that every time I see them I half think I hear the moan of the approaching & hovering shell & the black grisly flap that it seems to make as it bursts. I see & hear more than I did because changed conditions compel us to go up to the very front among the infantry to do our observation & we spend nights without shelter in the mud chiefly in waiting for morning & the arrival of the relief. It is a 24 hour job & takes more to recover from. But it is far as yet from being unendurable. The unendurable thing was having to climb up the inside of a chimney that was being shelled. I gave up. It was impossible & I knew it yet I went up to the beastly place & had 4 shell burst very close & decided that I would go back. As a matter of fact I had no light & no information about the method of getting up so that all the screwing up I had given myself would in any case have been futile. It was just another experience like the gamekeeper—but it lies far less on my mind, because the practical result of my failure was nil & I now see far more from the ground level than I could have seen then from 200 feet up the factory chimney.

Otherwise I have done all the things so far asked of me without making any mess & I have mingled satisfaction with dissatisfaction in about the usual proportion, comfort & discomfort. There are so many things to enjoy & if I remember rightly not more boredom than say a year or ten years ago. I think I get surer of some primitive things that one has got to get sure of, about myself & other people, & I think this is not due simply to being older. In short, I am glad I came out & I think less about return than I thought I should—partly no doubt I inhibit the idea of return. I only think by flashes of the things at home that I used to enjoy & should again—I enjoy many of them out here when the sun shines & at early morning & late afternoon. I doubt if anybody here thinks less of home than I do & yet I doubt if anybody loves it more.

But why should I be explaining myself at such length & not leave you to do the explaining?

We have shifted lately from the edge of a small city out to a still more ruinous village. The planks & beams of the ruins keep us warm in a house that has not had an actual hit except by fragments. We live in comparative comfort, eat luxuriously (from parcels sent from London or brought up from places well behind the line) & sleep dry & warm as a rule. We expect soon to have to live in damp dug outs for safety. There are some random shots but as a rule you know where to expect trouble & you can feel quite safe close to a place that is deadly dangerous. We work or make others work practically all day with no rests or holidays, but often we have a quiet evening & can bathe or write letters or listen to the gramophone playing "John Peel" & worse things far. People are mostly friendly & warm, however uncongenial. I am more than ten years older than 4 or out of the other 5 officers. They are 19, 20, 25, 26 & 33 years old. Those of 25 & 26 regard me as very old. I don't know if the two boys do—I get on better with them: in a sort of way we are fond of one another—I like to see them come in of a night back from some job & I believe they like to see me. What more should anyone want? I revert for 10 minutes every night by reading Shakespeare's Tragedies in bed with a pipe before I blow the candle out. Otherwise I do nothing that I used to do except eat & sleep: I mean when I am not alone. Funny world. What a thing it is.[1] And I hear nothing of you—yet you are no more like an American in a book than you were 2½ years ago. You are among the unchanged things that I can not or dare not think of except in flashes. I don't have memories except such as are involved in my impressions as I see or hear things about me. But if I went on writing like this I should make you think I was as damnably introspective as ever & practised the art too. Goodnight to you & Elinor & all. Remember I am in 244 Siege Battery, B. E. F., France & am & shall remain 2nd Lieut. Edward Thomas

Yours ever.

---

[1] Two sayings of David ("Dad") Uzzell, who was for Thomas a kind of paternal figure.

78. Frost to Helen Thomas

Amherst Mass
April 27 1917

Dear Helen:

People have been praised for self-possession in danger. I have heard Edward doubt if he was as brave as the bravest. But who was ever so completely himself right up to the verge of destruction, so sure of his thought, so sure of his word? He was the bravest and best and dearest man you and I have ever known. I knew from the moment when I first met him at his unhappiest that he would someday clear his mind and save his life. I have had four wonderful years with him. I know he has done this all for you: he's all yours. But you must let me cry my cry for him as if he were <u>almost</u> all mine too.

Of the three ways out of here, by death where there is no choice, by death where there is a noble choice, and by death where there is a choice not so noble, he found the greatest way. There is no regret—nothing that I will call a regret. Only I can't help wishing he could have saved his life without so wholly losing it and come back from France not too much hurt to enjoy our pride in him. I want to see him to tell him something. I want to tell him, what I think he liked to hear from me, that he was a poet. I want to tell him that I love those he loved and hate those he hated. (But the hating will wait: there will be a time for hate.) I had meant to talk endlessly with him still, either here in our mountains as we had said or, as I found my longing was more and more, there at Leddington where we first talked of war.

It was beautiful as he did it. And I don't suppose there is anything for us to do to show our admiration but to love him forever.

Robert

Other things for other letters.

79. Frost, "To E. T."[1]

To E. T.

I slumbered with your poems on my breast
Spread open as I dropped them half-read through
Like dove wings on a figure on a tomb
To see, if in a dream they brought of you,

I might not have the chance I missed in life
Through some delay, and call you to your face
First soldier, and then poet, and then both,
Who died a soldier-poet of your race.

I meant, you meant, that nothing should remain
Unsaid between us, brother, and this remained—
And one thing more that was not then to say:
The Victory for what it lost and gained.

You went to meet the shell's embrace of fire
On Vimy Ridge; and when you fell that day
The war seemed over more for you than me,
But now for me than you—the other way.

How over, though, for even me who knew
The foe thrust back unsafe beyond the Rhine,
If I was not to speak of it to you
And see you pleased once more with words of mine?

[1] First published in *The Yale Review*, April 1920, and later included in *New Hampshire* (1923).

80. Frost, "A Soldier"[1]

A Soldier

He is that fallen lance that lies as hurled,
That lies unlifted now, come dew, come rust,
But still lies pointed as it plowed the dust.
If we who sight along it round the world,
See nothing worthy to have been its mark,
It is because like men we look too near,
Forgetting that as fitted to the sphere,
Our missiles always make too short an arc.
They fall, they rip the grass, they intersect
The curve of the earth, and striking, break their own;
They make us cringe for metal-point on stone.
But this we know, the obstacle that checked
And tripped the body, shot the spirit on
Further than target ever showed or shone.

---

[1] First published as "The Soldier" in *McCalls*, May 1927, and later included in *West-Running Brook* (1928).

81. Frost, "Iris by Night"[1]

Iris by Night

One misty evening, one another's guide,
We two were groping down a Malvern side
The last wet fields and dripping hedges home.
There came a moment of confusing lights,
Such as according to belief in Rome
Were seen of old at Memphis on the heights
Before the fragments of a former sun
Could concentrate anew and rise as one.
Light was a paste of pigment in our eyes.
And then there was a moon and then a scene
So watery as to seem submarine;
In which we two stood saturated, drowned.
The clover-mingled rowan on the ground
Had taken all the water it could as dew,
And still the air was saturated too,
Its airy pressure turned to water weight.
Then a small rainbow like a trellis gate,
A very small moon-made prismatic bow,
Stood closely over us through which to go.
And then we were vouchsafed the miracle

---

[1] First published in the *Virginia Quarterly Review* (April 1936), but possibly written by 1929.
Included in *A Further Range* (1936). Compare Thomas's "The sun used to shine" [54].

That never yet to other two befell
And I alone of us have lived to tell.
A wonder! Bow and rainbow as it bent,
Instead of moving with us as we went,
(To keep the pots of gold from being found)
It lifted from its dewy pediment
Its two mote-swimming many-colored ends,
And gathered them together in a ring.
And we stood in it softly circled round
From all division time or foe can bring
In a relation of elected friends.

AFTERWORD

Twenty days after Thomas was killed at Arras, Frost wrote from Amherst: "Edward Thomas was the only brother I ever had." Frost liked to be literal-minded before becoming metaphorical-minded. He chose to speak the literal. He did have a sister, but "Edward Thomas was the only brother I ever had." Yet his words carry the further thought that such a friend may be more of a brother than any brother by blood. Tennyson, who had many brothers, never slighted family feeling, but he did feel a duty to speak the truth, and—of his dead friend Arthur Hallam—to breathe the words, "More than my brothers are to me." To say this (*In Memoriam* IX), and moreover to say it again, addressing on this second occasion his brother Charles:

> 'More than my brothers are to me,'
> Let this not vex thee, noble heart! (LXXIX)

Frost and Thomas were brothers. They were not to be brothers-in-arms, but they were brothers-in-arts. And this without sibling rivalry, despite their belonging to the irritable tribe of scribblers, those who so often—as Pope wrote of the competitive man of letters, Joseph Addison ("A tim'rous foe, and a suspicious friend")—will

> Bear, like the Turk, no brother near the throne,
> View him with scornful, yet with jealous eyes,
> And hate for arts that caus'd himself to rise;

> *Damn with faint praise, assent with civil leer,*
> *And without sneering, teach the rest to sneer.* (*Epistle to Dr. Arbuthnot*)

Frost was to find himself having to tell Thomas that the Americans had turned down "Four and Twenty Blackbirds," retailing "the praise our publishers damned it with" (28 September 1916). England and America, sharing a mother-tongue, have always had their sibling rivalries. An acknowledgment of this history can be felt to stir as Frost goes on to say more:

> Edward Thomas was the only brother I ever had. I fail to see how we can have been so much to each other, he an Englishman and I an American and our first meeting put off till we were both in middle life.
>
> (To Edward Garnett, 29 April 1917)

What staves off sentimentality is the idiom *I fail to see*, which in the ordinary way is never an admission of failure at all; on the contrary, it truculently insists that someone else has failed to see the true state of affairs: I fail to see how you can suppose for a moment that there is anything to be said for what you are saying . . . When Frost uses this idiom, it therefore brings in something more than (though nothing less than) the simple loving sense, *I shall always marvel at how we can have been so much to each other*, in that it conveys a sense of how much could so easily have set them ("he an Englishman and I an American") at a distance or at odds. I fail to see by what right the English are so goddamn condescending, or the Americans so damnably hail-fellow-well-met.

In their letters (do any of their poems ever house *both* countries?), America and England are much mentioned. But those very different dwelling places, New Hampshire and Hampshire (Thomas, 19 May 1914: "I hardly expect it of New Hampshire more than of old"), are not dwelt upon. Despite the present years in England that were realized by Frost and despite the future years in America that Thomas was never to realize, neither Frost nor Thomas felt obliged to pronounce upon the characteristics, leave alone the long-standing shortcomings, of either country, to promulgate an idea of the English or the Americans, whether a right or a wrong idea. Frost will report to Thomas that a friend "had a pleasant talk with me on English traits peculiarities idiosyncracies etc." (17 April 1915)— but "I would not have him run off with the idea that because I poked a little fun at Wilfrid [Gibson] I am no lover of the English," adding with a waggish finger "—when they [are] right."

My country, right or wrong? Presumably not. Your country, right or wrong? Certainly not. Thomas had always responded in kindliness.

> I like the photographs. Some of them were almost a pleasant shock after what I imagined probable in your country (and here for that matter). I wish I knew that I would see that country. (24 February 1914)

This is rueful, but it does not rue anything about your country— or mine, really: "(and here for that matter)". Frost:

> Old Lynch hates England but entertains no nonsense as to what would happen if Germany won. Every Yankee in America (practically) wants England to win—England and France. (17 April 1915)

It is good to be reminded that not every American is a Yankee, and that a man whose name is Lynch may have good old emerald reasons for hating England and may even have a wrong idea of England.

Three months before Frost and Thomas first met on 6 October 1913, Elinor Frost wrote to Sidney Cox:

> The English have such a wrong idea of America, but you couldn't expect anything else from the sort of American news that gets printed in the papers here; anything vulgar and sensational about us is welcomed, and only confirms what they had already thought of us. (10 July 1913)

Two months after Frost and Thomas first met, Frost found himself up against an English review by John Alford that tackled sixteen books of American poetry, a review that is very sure what it is just as well to state about the United States.

Alford:

> Now it is just as well to state at the beginning that I can find no support to a belief that there is any such thing as American poetry; just as an examination of the Metropolitan Museum of New York finally destroyed my idea that there was any such thing as American art.

Frost:

> This is what makes it impossible that I should live long under a criss-cross flag. Me of the three colors the bluebird wears. This cub doesn't know how to find his way around among American writers. No one he mentions is thought anything of on the other side—no one of recent date.
>
> (to John T. Bartlett, circa 15 December 1913)

No one, except that Alford judged it prudent to make an exception, the better to curl his lip more largely: "Mr. Pound is a unique phenomenon, for he has succeeded in being an American, a man of culture and a poet, all at the same time."

So that when, in a review in the *Daily News* (22 July 1914), Thomas praises those successes of Frost that put him "above all other writers of verse in America," it may need to be recalled that for many contemporaries in England this could have been misconstrued as damning with praise so faint as to be, paradoxically, a hoot.

Frost, for the good reason that he knew both countries well, was more willing than Thomas to venture judgments thereabouts, such as in his apprehensions of "All the follies that England is like to die of" (26 June 1915). But he is wary of sounding forth as the voice of America, so he chooses to avail himself of a slightly different sense of things from that of his wife, perhaps, or to have recourse to the handy Americanism, "I sort of": "Elinor is afraid the rawness of these back towns will be too much for you. You know I sort of like it." Either way (and the phrase that he proceeds to use does convey an either-way), "It is really the Hell of a country."

For real Hell, there would prove to be the trenches. Such was the choice that had just been made by Thomas. "These last few days I have been looking at 2 alternatives, trying to enlist or coming out to America" (18 June 1915). Less than a month later, the choice of life—which proved to be a choice of death—had been made: "Last week I had screwed myself up to the point of believing I should come out to America & lecture if anyone wanted me to. But I have altered my mind. I am going to enlist on Wednesday if the doctor will pass me. I am aiming at the 'Artists Rifles', a territorial battalion, chiefly for training officers" (11 July 1915). "Aiming at": this levels its sights. As to his greater territorial battalion, his native land, Thomas was not disillusioned, all things considered, but unillusioned he was. He had had to work so despairingly hard in order to scrape a living with his pen. After speaking of "the extent to which my earning in general was declining," he came to a grim conclusion: "My country had virtually deserted me before I decided not to desert it" (28 August 1915). And he chose to put it like this at a time when the verb *to desert* had a somber weight to it, especially for someone who had enlisted. He who fights, and runs away, lives to fight another day. And in the long run? There was to be no such run or running for Thomas. He did not look forward, exactly.

I don't look ahead with any anxiety. I just look forward without a thought to something, I don't know what, I don't speculate what. But I can tell you that the only element I am conscious of when I look forward is New Hampshire. I realize—I think no more about it—that England will be no place for me when all is over, though of course things may happen.

(13 November 1915)

Things happened, and when all was over, no place was to be his. Each was afraid that the other—and the other's work—might find itself misrepresented, not as too American in the one case and too English in the other, but in both cases as too English. Frost:

> am I now going to tell you in cold writing that I tried to place your 'Four-and-twenty Blackbirds' with Holt and failed. I know it was something I didn't say or do to bear down the publishers doubts of the book as too English for the American mother and child. It is not too English.
>
> (23 November 1915)

Conversely, or versely, Thomas had specified the objection to Garnett's article on Frost in *The Atlantic*: "that it reminds people you were over here & gives you a shade too much of English in your composition" (4 October 1915). Composition, as what makes up both Frost and Frost's writing.

Frost, who both liked and loved Thomas, understood the further damage done by war.

> I'm afraid Englishmen aren't liking Americans very much just now. Should I dare to go back to England at this moment? I often long to. The hardest part of it would be to be treated badly for what is none of my fault personally.
>
> (28 September 1916)

Thomas, who both liked and loved Frost, never treated him badly by assimilating him, personally, to any national character, let alone caricature. Thomas always saw Frost as an American, while never seeing him as the American, or as like an American put down in a book. In his last letter to Frost, a week before Thomas was killed, he wrote with sadness and with the deepest of gratitude:

> And I hear nothing of you—yet you are no more like an American in a book than you were 2½ years ago. You are among the unchanged things that I can not or dare not think of except in flashes.
>
> (2 April 1917)

Of *North of Boston*, Thomas wrote: "Few that read it through will have been as much astonished by any American since Whitman" (*The New Weekly*, 8 August 1914). One cause of mild astonishment might have been Frost's being perfectly at home with the verse-line that announced, or that seemed to many Americans to announce (as Whitman's lines are far from announcing), *Englishness*. What Thomas, in praising Frost here, calls "the good old English medium of blank verse" was starting to seem not at all a good old medium— being English—to the new American modernists whose sport was throwing the shackle. When Thomas respects Frost's having "chosen the unresisting medium of blank verse," we might remember the resistance that was setting itself to fight this colonialist invader.

"To break the pentameter, that was the first heave." These were the terms in which Pound was to look back from the vantage point of *The Cantos* (Canto 81). The personal may or may not be the political, but the new American poetry would be in no doubt that the metrical is the political. For Frost, though, there was no reason why New England need fear being oppressed by the prosody of old England.

Frost, who wrote such entirely American books, was not himself like an American in a book. And the books by the Englishman who put it like that, were they too English? Frost, to whom blaming himself did not come easily or factitiously, blamed himself for having failed to move the American publishers from their "doubts of the book as too English for the American mother and child. It is not too English" (23 November 1915). The publishers proffered another epithet, one that was by way of being a synonym for "English."

I failed in a way that was no discredit to you with the 'Four and Twenty Blackbirds'. "Too insular" was the praise our publishers damned it with for American purposes.   (28 September 1916)

Too insular, too English: too Engsular, in short.

It was in the previous year, as Henry James watched the war, that he suddenly realized the positive force of what had become a negative word, "insular." In "Within the Rim," an essay written in 1915 and published in 1917, James pondered "the English character" and "the genius of the race."

> "Insularity!"—one had spent no small part of one's past time in mocking or in otherwise fingering the sense out of that word; yet here it was in the air wherever one looked and as stuffed with meaning as if nothing had ever worn away from it, as if its full force on the contrary amounted to inward congestion. What the term essentially signified was in the oddest way a question at once enormous and irrelevant; what it might *show* as signifying, what it was in the circumstances actively and most probably going to, seemed rather the true consideration, indicated with all the weight of the evidence scattered about. Just the fixed *look* of England under the August sky, what was this but the most vivid exhibition of character conceiveable . . . ?[1]

In the days of wars that were fought by land and sea, not by air, England thanked its lucky stars—there being as yet no disastrous Star Wars—for its security as a right little, tight little, island. From Land's End to John o' Groats, or to John of Gaunt:

> This royal throne of kings, this scepter'd isle,
> This earth of majesty, this seat of Mars,
> This other Eden, demi-paradise,
> This fortress built by Nature for herself
> Against infection and the hand of war,
> This happy breed of men, this little world,
> This precious stone set in the silver sea,
> Which serves it in the office of a wall,

---

[1] *Within the Rim and Other Essays 1914–15* (1918), pp. 23–4.

> Or as a moat defensive to a house,
> Against the envy of less happier lands,
> This blessed plot, this earth, this realm, this England . . .

The poet who was thought in America to be "too insular" was the author of "This England" (7 November 1914), and the editor of *This England: An Anthology from Her Writers* (1915).

It was only with the uninvaded peace of the eighteenth century that "insular" had come to be a word of reproach:

> Pertaining to islanders; *esp.* having the characteristic traits of the inhabitants of an island (e.g., of Great Britain); cut off from intercourse with other nations, isolated; self-contained; narrow or prejudiced in feelings, ideas, or manners.   (*Oxford English Dictionary*, 4a.)

The first instance (1775) is from Dr. Johnson, who was himself not without prejudice when it came to these Western Islands of Scotland.

A war makes people think about themselves as a people. They become rightly conscious of their nationality; sometimes this makes them nationalists, sometimes internationalists, but always there is a heightened sense of just what it means, and should mean, to belong to a nation. It was during the Great War that James—an American long domiciled in England—decided to become a British citizen. The author of *The Europeans* was a true European. In the words of another American who was to take British citizenship:

> It is the final perfection, the consummation of an American to become, not an Englishman, but a European—something which no born European, no person of any European nationality, can become.
> (T. S. Eliot, "In Memory of Henry James", *Egoist*, January 1918)

To disparage Thomas, there had come to mind and to hand the word "insular." To disparage Frost, there might be "provincial."

But as with "insular," a rescue operation could be mounted. T. S. Eliot reviewed the *Letters of Mrs. Gaskell and Charles Eliot Norton, 1855–1865*, and after noting flatly that "Neither Norton nor Mrs. Gaskell, seventeen years his senior, was a European," Eliot decided to end the review by putting in a word for the word "provincial": "she is among those English (and American) writers who have known how to make a literary virtue out of provinciality—and, in her case, simple goodness" (*New England Quarterly*, September 1933).

Frost knew how to make a great many literary virtues out of provinciality. Or, if the scale were allowed to become even more local, out of the parochial, the parish pump (the local or the parochial, says the dictionary). Pound did his best to parish-pump up the volume. The volume was *North of Boston*, published in London. Published in Chicago, Pound's review in *Poetry* opened:

> It is a sinister thing that so American, I might even say so parochial, a talent as that of Robert Frost should have to be exported before it can find due encouragement and recognition.   (December 1914)

Frost himself had written, the previous year, "These Englishmen are very charming. I begin to think I shall stay with them till I'm deported" (to Thomas Mosher, 24 October 1913). But the joke about deported is one thing, and Pound's *exported*, another. Expat. exported? Since publication in London did not seem to Frost a sinister thing, he found Pound gauche, or out in left field:

> The harm he does lies in this: he made up his mind in the short time I was friends with him (we quarreled in six weeks) to add me to his party of American literary refugees in London. Nothing could be more unfair, nothing better calculated to make me an exile for life. Another such review as the one in Poetry and I shan't be admitted at Ellis Island. This is no joke. Since the article was published I have been insulted and snubbed by two American editors I counted on as good friends. I dont repine and

I am willing to wait for justice. But I do want someone to know that I am not a refugee and I am not in any way disloyal. My publishing a book in England was as it happened.   (to Sidney Cox, 2 January 1915)

The life of a wit, said Pope, is a warfare upon earth. In 1915, the warfare was bloodier than any bookish battle of the ancients and the modernists. In time of the breaking of nations, refugees were flesh and blood. Next year, Henry James published in the *Times Literary Supplement* his pity and indignation, "Refugees in Chelsea."

Ezra Pound can be taken as the third term in all this, the term that may help us to get purchase on the other two, who were not short-time friends but long-time ones. Pound never had any patience for Thomas, though patience was one of Thomas's greatest glories. (He wrote to Frost, 5 March 1916: "No one can have Patience who pursues Glory, so you will have to toss up with Eleanor which vice you shall claim in public.") Thomas was "a mild fellow with no vinegar in his veins," according to Pound, who was a wild fellow with so much vinegar in his veins as to seem not so much full-blooded as full-vinegared.[2] The mild fellow, who later came to think ill of himself for having spoken too well of Pound, had reviewed him three times in 1909 and once in 1910, with caveats but plaudits.

Carelessness of sweet sound and of all the old tricks makes Mr Pound's book rather prickly to handle at first. It was practically nothing but this prickliness that incited us to read his book through a second time. We read it a third time—it is less than sixty pages long—because it was good the second, and, nevertheless, still held back other good things.

(reviewing *Personae* in the *Daily Chronicle*, 7 June 1909)

---

[2] A remark made to Richard J. Stonesifer (see his *W. H. Davies: A Critical Biography*, 1963, p. 239), quoted in *A Language Not to Be Betrayed: Selected Prose of Edward Thomas*, ed. Edna Longley (1981), p. xii.

This is firm praise, praise that was not to be held back, in its admiration of such poems as do the good thing of conveying that they are holding back further good things. Thomas, as reader and as critic, was always consistent in his principles, and what went for his reading of Pound would in due course go for his reading of Frost. 19 October 1916: "I like nearly everything of yours better at a 2nd reading & best after that. True." There was never a man who less needed to offer the assurance, after saying such a thing, that it was true.

It was in 1913 that Frost and Thomas met. It was in 1913 that Frost met a reviewer's assurance that "Mr. Pound is a unique phenomenon, for he has succeeded in being an American, a man of culture and a poet, all at the same time." It was in 1913 that Pound (in London) noticed Frost:

> There is another personality in the realm of verse, another American, found, as usual, on this side of the water, by an English publisher long known as a lover of good letters. David Nutt publishes at his own expense A Boy's Will, by Robert Frost, the latter having been long scorned by the 'great American editors'. It is the old story.
>
> (The New Freewoman, September 1913)

And it was in 1913 that Pound wrote—and sent to the publisher (it finally achieved publication in 1950)—his study of his native land, an essay to which he gave a title, *Patria Mia*, that was couched in the language of a land that he was both to honor and to dishonor in a later war: Italy.

> I trust in the national chemical, or, if the reader be of Victorian sensibility, let us say the 'spirit' or the 'temper' of the nation.

I have found in 'The Seafarer' and in 'The Wanderer' trace of what I should call the English national chemical. In those early Anglo-Saxon poems I find expression of that quality which seems to me to have transformed the successive arts of poetry that have been brought to England from the South. For the art has come mostly from the south, and it has found on the island something in the temper of the race which has strengthened it and given it fibre. And this is hardly more than a race conviction that words scarcely become a man.

> "Nor may the weary-in-mind withstand his fate,
> Nor is high heart his helping.
> For the doom-eager oft bindeth fast his thought in
> blood-bedabbled breast."

The word I have translated 'doom-eager' is 'domgeorne'. And 'dom' is both 'fate' and 'glory'. The 'Dom georne' man is the man ready for his deed, eager for it, eager for the glory of it, ready to pay the price.

If a man has this quality and be meagre of speech one asks little beyond this.

I find the same sort of thing in Whitman. I mean I find in him what I should be as ready to call our American keynote as I am to call this the English keynote.

It is, as nearly as I can define it, a certain generosity; a certain carelessness, or looseness, if you will; a hatred of the sordid, an ability to forget the part for the sake of the whole, a desire for largeness, a willingness to stand exposed.

> 'Camerado, this is no book;
> Who touches this touches a man.'

The artist is ready to endure personally a strain which his craftsmanship would scarcely endure.

Here is a spirit, one might say, as hostile to the arts as was the Anglo-Saxon objection to speaking at all.

Yet the strength of both peoples is just here; that one undertakes to keep quiet until there is something worth saying, and the other will undertake nothing in its art for which it will not be in person responsible.

(1962 ed., pp. 44–6)

One of the strengths shared by Frost and Thomas is their each combining, in different proportions, the national chemicals, English and American, on which Pound had speculated. *A race conviction that words scarcely become a man. A willingness to stand exposed.* Thomas had praised such a voice as was capable of "expressing likes and dislikes right out of his heart, without any of the hesitation which I have so often that I really never ought to say or write anything."[3] Frost praised Thomas for being—in his decision to enlist—a man of words and of deeds, a man of his word, a man "so sure of his word" (as Frost was later to say in his letter of condolence to Helen Thomas, 27 April 1917).

You are doing it for the self-same reason I shall hope to do it for if my time ever comes and I am brave enough, namely, because there seems nothing else for a man to do. (31 July 1915)

Frost, aware of the geographical distance and of the human closeness, knew that (at such a time) words scarcely became a man:

I have stopped asseverating from a sense of fitness. You rather shut me up by enlisting. Talk is almost too cheap when all your friends are facing bullets. I don't believe I ought to enlist (since I am of course an American), but if I can't enlist, at least I refuse to talk sympathy beyond a certain point. (6 November 1916)

And Thomas, who was never more humane than when, in replying, he declined to retort, was grateful not only for these words

---

[3] Above, p. xv. *Selected Letters*, p. 45.

but for the words of the poem in which Frost declined to word the war away. The poem, "Suggested by Talk of Peace at This Time," was never published by Frost, perhaps because he took with more seriousness even than usual his words "Not mine to say. . . ."

> France, France, I know not what is in my heart.
> But God forbid that I should be more brave
> As watcher from a quiet place apart
> Than you are fighting in an open grave.
>
> Not mine to say you shall not think of peace.
> Not mine, not mine: I almost know your pain.

Thomas, who knew the pain of the war, knew what it was his to say:

> I had your letter & your poem "France, France" yesterday. I like the poem very much, because it betrays exactly what you *would* say & what you feel about saying that much. It expresses just those hesitations you or I would have at asking others to act as we think it is their cue to act. Well, I am soon going to know more about it. (31 December 1916)

Thomas, who sought to use "A language not to be betrayed" (this, from the poem "I Never Saw that Land Before"), knew too the uses of such a language as betrays exactly what you *would* say and what you feel about saying that much. And "asking others to act as we think it is their cue to act": in Pound's understanding,

> the strength of both peoples is just here; that one undertakes to keep quiet until there is something worth saying, and the other will undertake nothing in its art for which it will not be in person responsible.

———

Though friendship is what these letters and poems breathe, it is not often what they use their breath to talk about. Moreover, these highly intelligent friends are intelligent about friendship, about the threat that sentimentality or other forms of self-deception may pose to it. Unrequited love exists, but there is no such thing as unrequited friendship—and since we rightly set such store by friendship, it is ripe for such fantasies as Proust set himself to scrutinize. Neither Frost nor Thomas is ever cynical about friendship, but their scepticism has its health. There are friends, and friends.

Thomas: "So I pester my friends, or did when I had such" (13 June 1915). Frost: "Some of my friends will be good to you. Some of them aren't good to me even. That is to say they persist in liking me for the wrong reasons and in otherwise disregarding my wishes" (26 June 1915).

Frost, resisting the burliness of others: "I have been spoiled by a mob of new friends who don't care what becomes of me so long as they get my autograph once in so often" (15 August 1916). Thomas, resisting any misrepresenting of himself by himself:

There is nobody I like much, that is the worst of it. I don't want friends. I don't think I should like to have friends out here. I am sure I shouldn't. But I want companions & I hardly expect to find them. This may not be final. There are plenty of likable people. (6 March 1917)

The loveliest and most loving thing that Thomas ever said to Frost says nothing of friendship while conveying everything of it: "The next best thing to having you here is having the space (not a void) that nobody else can fill" (4 October 1915). It was left to Frost, left widowered in friendship (as Tennyson felt himself to have been), to evoke in absence the enduring closeness. "I don't know that I ever told you," he wrote to Amy Lowell on October 22, 1917, "but the closest I ever came in friendship to anyone in England or anywhere else in the world I think was with Edward Thomas who was killed at Vimy last spring." Not the closest he ever came *to* friendship, but the closest he ever came *in* friendship.

In their art, both Frost and Thomas enjoyed the conditions in which rhymes were friends, not only friends to the poets' art but friends to one another, to their fellow-rhymes. Rhyme is like friendship in that it is only by being reciprocated that it constitutes rhyme. True, there are poems in which the rhymes are pitched against one another, frictive or fractious, but such was very seldom Frost's style and was perhaps never Thomas's. Not that friendship will always get its way. On the contrary, it may—among all the other losses including the final one—lose its way. It is characteristic of Thomas's art, in its imagining friendship, that it should guard against sentimentality, again, by treating the word "friends" differently from any other rhyme to which the poem turns.

"The Bridge"

I have come a long way today:
On a strange bridge alone,
Remembering friends, old friends,
I rest, without smile or moan,
As they remember me without smile or moan.

All are behind, the kind
And the unkind too, no more
To-night than a dream. The stream
Runs softly yet drowns the Past,
The dark-lit stream has drowned the Future and the Past.

No traveller has rest more blest
Than this moment brief between
Two lives, when the Night's first lights
And shades hide what has never been,
Things goodlier, lovelier, dearer, than will be or have been.

"The Bridge" has internal rhymes in the first and third lines of its stanzas. In the second stanza, *behind/kind*, and *dream/stream*. In the third stanza, *rest/blest*, and *Night's/lights*. But in the first stanza, *way/today* is followed by *friend/friend*. "Remembering friends, old friends." Entirely a rhyme and not a rhyme at all. The rhyme-word remembers not another but itself, in a moment that muses in the stasis of pathos. "On a strange bridge alone": and "friends" finds itself alone, and all the more alone for being a plural that then occurs plurally.

This is the art of someone who values friendship because he weighs it, Thomas, who evoked his friend Frost within the poem "A Dream":

> Over known fields with an old friend in dream
> I walked, but came sudden to a strange stream.

As in "The Bridge," *dream* is duly joined in rhyme by *stream* (likewise in the neighborhood of "strange"). But "an old friend" does not come to be rhymed, even with itself as it had been in "The Bridge" ("Remembering friends, old friends"). Or rather is not yet, in "A Dream," joined in rhyme. For the final sentence of "A Dream" will come to embrace this rhyme of *friend* with *end* that is not forgotten by poets:

> So by the roar and hiss
> And by the mighty motion of the abyss
> I was bemused, that I forgot my friend
> And neither saw nor sought him till the end,
> When I awoke from waters unto men
> Saying: 'I shall be here some day again.'

Bemused, benignly, because befriended by the muse.

Thomas was darkly pleased to play serious games with the word "friend" and the rhyming company that it might keep. There is the internal interplay of "the end" with "friendship" in the opening stanza of "Home," for instance, or (yet more somberly) the end of "Old Man," a poem that ends with the word "end," a black-and-black negative of a scene that lacks all memories, including that of a friend with whom to rhyme:

> No garden appears, no path, no hoar-green bush
> Of Lad's-love, or Old Man, no child beside,
> Neither father nor mother, nor any playmate;
> Only an avenue, dark, nameless, without end.

This is all the more poignant because there at the end of the penultimate line, positioned with at least the imaginability of a rhyme, there is the absent playmate, who might in some other world have been a friend:

> Neither father nor mother, nor any friend;
> Only an avenue, dark, nameless, without end.

Yet that is a phantom friend of a rhyme, whereas *friend/end* is tangibly there elsewhere in Thomas, as it is Frost:

"Revelation"

> We make ourselves a place apart
>   Behind light words that tease and flout,
> But oh, the agitated heart
>   Till someone really find us out.
>
> 'Tis pity if the case require
>   (Or so we say) that in the end
> We speak the literal to inspire
>   The understanding of a friend.

> But so with all, from babes that play
>   At hide-and-seek to God afar,
> So all who hide too well away
>   Must speak and tell us where they are.

From *A Boy's Will* (1915), where the next poem, "The Trial by Existence," likewise rhymes *end/friend*.

But the Frost poem that most matters here and now is the one that celebrates the enduring friendship of Thomas and Frost, more than twenty years after they met for the last time, "Iris by Night." The messenger of the gods brings her rainbow-sign, in the poem's lasting conclusion:

> And then we were vouchsafed the miracle
> That never yet to other two befell
> And I alone of us have lived to tell.
> A wonder! Bow and rainbow as it bent,
> Instead of moving with us as we went,
> (To keep the pots of gold from being found)
> It lifted from its dewy pediment
> Its two mote-swimming many-colored ends,
> And gathered them together in a ring.
> And we stood in it softly circled round
> From all division time or foe can bring
> In a relation of elected friends.

These lines gather together in a ring so much that Thomas and Frost were loyal to, not only their friendship with one another, but their friendship with the poems that circled them round. There is Shelley, with his sense of loss at the death of Keats, who yet was never a friend:

> The One remains, the many change and pass;
> Heaven's light forever shines, Earth's shadows fly;

Life, like a dome of many-coloured glass,
Stains the white radiance of Eternity,
Until Death tramples it to fragments.   *(Adonais)*

To the making of what is in effect one section of Frost's *In Memoriam E. T.*, there goes *In Memoriam A. H. H.*, which had balanced grief and happiness nearly twenty years after Tennyson last met his friend:

> *And in that solace can I sing,*
> *Till out of painful phases wrought*
> *There flutters up a happy thought*
> *Self-balanced on a lightsome wing:*
>
> *Since we deserved the name of friends,*
> *And thine effect so lives in me,*
> *A part of mine may live in thee*
> *And move thee on to noble ends.*   (the end of In Memoriam LXV)

"The name of friends,/And thine effect . . .": friends effected, and unaffectedly affected, elected friends. Tennyson—in a setting that, like that of "Iris by Night," obliquely invokes light and directly evokes what it is to *live* and *move*—brings it about that friends meet with noble ends. Yet Frost, unlike Tennyson, lets "friends" both be and have the last word, within this rhyme that Thomas and he and their many predecessors shared.

> *And we stood in it softly circled round*
> *From all division time or foe can bring*
> *In a relation of elected friends.*

Frost's happy thought, self-balanced on a lightsome ring, encircles so many relations. Here are "elected friends," yet not by the prissy lights of Samuel Rowlands in 1607:

A heedful care we ought to have,
When we do friends elect.

For Frost's "elected" is electrically charged with its affinities to "elective," and so with all the elective affinities that move Goethe and that then moved so many others, including Oliver Wendell Holmes. Frost's use of "elected" in the immediate vicinity of his vision of miraculous light is illuminated by "elective." In "Iris by Night," light is the element, as it had been in James Hutton's *Upon the philosophy of light, heat and fire* (1794), "The elective affections of this irradiated influence," or in Tyndall's *Light* (1869), light sifted by "elective absorption."

(*Chem.*): the tendency of a substance to combine with certain particular substances in preference to others.

Such are these preferences that are more than preferences. In *Middlemarch*, a man exclaims in anger: "Explain my preference! I never had a *preference* for her, any more than I have a preference for breathing."

"You please yourself. I should prefer the truth
Or nothing. Here, in fact, is nothing at all
Except a silent place that once rang loud,
And trees and us—imperfect friends, we men
And trees since time began; and nevertheless
Between us still we breed a mystery."

(Thomas, the end of "The Chalk-Pit")

Imperfect friends, we men and trees, but friends nevertheless. Never the less of a mystery was the perfect friendship of Edward Thomas and Robert Frost, "a relation of elected friends" that it befell Frost—"And I alone of us have lived to tell"—to relate.

Christopher Ricks